INTERNATIONAL COMMUNICATION

By the Same Author

Communication Planning for Socio-Economic Development (edited with *Ranjit Singh*)

Media and Development : Themes in Communication and Extension. (edited with *M.R. Dua)*

Third Revolution in Indian Perspective – Contemporary Issues and Themes in Communication

Rural Press – Problems and Prospects, (edited with *Rajeshwar Dyal*)

Media Policy and Nation Building – Select Issues and Themes (with *Vir Bala Aggarwal*)

National Media Policy (edited with *Rajeshwar Dyal*)

Media and Market Forces – Challenges and Opportunities (edited with *Rajeshwar Dyal*)

Communication Technology, Media Policy and National Development

Communication and Development – The Challenge of the Twenty-First Century

Handbook of Journalism and Mass Communication (with *Vir Bala Aggarwal*)

Handbook of Reporting and Communication Skills : Companion volume to Handbook of Journalism and Mass Communication

Communication, Development and Civil Society

About The Author

V.S. Gupta, a senior media and communication academic is a former professor, Haryana Agricultural University. A recipient of several awards and fellowships, Professor Gupta conceptualised and implemented a number of training programmes in development journalism and communication and reporting skills in the University.

As a country representative for the Asian Media, Information and Communication Centre (AMIC), Singapore, for a number of years, he organised numerous seminars and colloquial throughout the country. He has written and edited eleven books and a number of manuals, besides having been widely published in India and abroad.

Professor Gupta lives in UK and can be accessed at vijaya06102003@yahoo.co.uk

INTERNATIONAL COMMUNICATION

Contemporary Issues and Trends in Global Information Revolution

V.S. Gupta

CONCEPT PUBLISHING COMPANY, NEW DELHI-110059

Cataloging in Publication Data—DK
Courtesy: D.K. Agencies (P) Ltd. <docinfo@dkagencies.com>

Gupta, V. S. (Vijaya Sunder), 1940-
International communication : contemporary issues and trends in global information revolution / V.S. Gupta.
p. cm.
Includes bibliographical references (p.)
Includes index.
ISBN 8180692086

1. Communication, International. 2. Communication—Technological innovations. 3. Information technology. I. Title.

DDC 004.6 21

ISBN 81-8069-209-4 (P.B.)

First Published 2005

Published and Printed by
Ashok Kumar Mittal
Concept Publishing Company
A/15-16, Commercial Block, Mohan Garden,
New Delhi-110 059 (India)

Phones : 25351460, 25351794
Fax : 091-11-25357103
Email : publishing@conceptpub.com

PREFACE

During my UNDP fellowship for training in the audio-visual aids technology at the International Centre for Technical Vocational Training, Turin in 1976, I asked my German instructor P Gustave to recommend a number of books to keep me updated on issues of contemporary interest. The first book he recommended was the *Future Shock.* I purchased a copy of that book from Foyles at Oxford Street, London, which at that time was famed to be one of the largest book stores in the world. *Future Shock* and subsequently *Third Wave,* by Alvin Toffler remain two of the most heavily underlined and well-thumbed books in my personal library. These two books introduced me, for the first time, to the emerging trends in the world beyond my call of duty.

My association with the Asian Media Information and Communication Centre, Singapore, for the first time as a participant in a Media Seminar in Singapore in 1986, and subsequently my close association with the organisation as a Zonal and Country representative in India for a number of years; and also as an organiser of its conferences and seminars, gave me valuable insight into several aspects of media in a wider perspective. AMIC publications including issues of *Media Asia* on information technology, globalisation of news, human rights and right to information as well as on other subjects helped me acquire a body of literature of lasting value.

Therefore, in September 2003, when I and my wife Ramesh decided to live in UK, I took it upon myself the pending task of completing the book on international communication because the ambience for pursuing academic work has been quite conducive. The large number of books on sociology (of which media is a part), journals and newspapers available in the Slough Central Library, formed the core of my source material.

The UK online centres in the town and the easy accessibility of internet to search material made my task easier. It is for the first time I realised that with the advent of the internet, sources of references have multiplied rapidly, though selection, documentation, analysis and perspective still continue to be a daunting task for bringing out a proper book.

The book has been written keeping in view the requirement of the students studying International Communication as part of MA (Communication); as per the guidelines suggested by the Curriculum Development Committee of the University Grants Commission, and also for the NET examination.

It is essentially a documentation which attempts to present an analysis of the trends and developments in the current global media situation. It aims to provide a resource for the students and help them develop a sense of how these issues and trends are impacting our world. It is hoped that the book helps media scholars in the development of critical appreciation of these issues.

While writing this book, I have tried to use the latest knowledge and information available on the subject. The books and the websites consulted have been referred to in the text and also listed in the bibliography. I must place on record my deep debt of gratitude to all these authors whose work has helped me greatly in completing my task.

A list of ten recommended texts has been included in the bibliography for the guidance of the students who wish to study the subject further. By its very nature, international communication has become interdisciplinary, where knowledge of contemporary affairs, international economic and political developments and trends has become basic to the understanding of the subject.

As always, I warmly look forward to suggestions from the students and faculty for the improvement of the book, which will be incorporated in the subsequent editions.

V.S. GUPTA

ACKNOWLEDGEMENTS

This book was completed during my stay in UK, where I have had the academic resources of the Slough Central Library at my disposal, enjoyed the goodwill and support of friends and assistance from competent professionals.

I, therefore, owe a deep debt of gratitude to:

- The staff of the Slough Central Library and particularly to Gaynor Baveystock, Principal Librarian, Inclusion and Learning; for creating an ambience suitable for academic work;
- Cllr. Mewa S. Mann, former Mayor, Slough Borough Council, whose contribution to the civic life of the town remains unmatched and who holds several offices of honour as Vice President, British Indian Councillors Association, Heathrow Consultative Committee and Berkshire Community Trust; for all his help and goodwill; and
- Neeraj Goel Mittal, a Senior Software Professional, now pursuing her career in UK, Barbara Dodgson, our computer instructor, and Afsheen Lodhi, co-ordinator - Library Learn - UK Online Centre; for their assistance in researching and formatting the material.

I express my gratitude to all who form a part of my institutional, professional and personal network and who have, in various ways, contributed to my work as an academic and author. I place on record my sense of gratefulness to the following institutions, professional bodies and individuals:

- Haryana Agricultural University, which nominated me for UNDP fellowship in Turin and assigned me the responsibility of running two courses in development journalism, and communication and reporting skills,

– Asian Media Information and Communication Centre, Singapore, and its former Secretary General, Mr. Vijay Menon, for enabling me to build insights in communication problems and trends, and
– Several Universities and professional institutions, where I worked as visiting professor and was associated with their academic, curriculum development and research programmes. Some of these institutions and persons are: the departments of journalism at Himachal Pradesh University, Shimla, and its Head of the Department, Vir Bala Aggarwal, Kurukshetra University, Kurukshetra; Press Institute of India and the Indian Institute of Mass Communication, both in New Delhi; and the Indian Institute of Advanced Studies, Shimla.
– And finally, to Mr. Ashok Mittal, the publisher, for his interest, encouragement and suggestions in seeing the book through.

V.S. GUPTA
e-mail:vijaya06102003@yahoo.co.uk

CONTENTS

1
INTRODUCTION AND OVERVIEW

A text book on international communication, by the very nature of the subject, must refer to the trends in the contemporary global society. And at a time when the world is witnessing virtual revolution in almost every aspect of our lives; how does one describe the on-going situation:

- Runaway World
- Global Shift
- War and Anti-war, or simply
- Globalisation

Interestingly, these phrases not only depict essential trends and developments in the modern society, these are the titles of the books written during the recent past. Another book, *Tell Me Lies*, published in 2004 relates to media distortion in the context of attack on Iraq about which there has been saturated media coverage in the world press.

There has been a revolution in the air, which one can feel and breathe—fall of the Berlin Wall, collapse of the Soviet Union and the communist system, advent of global television and the World Wide Web, impacting the very way we watch and receive world events as these unfold themselves before our very eyes. We do not read history any more: either we "watch" history happening alongside with our morning cup of coffee, or we "surf" history.

How does one capture the sense, the excitement and the import of these events and trends, still developing and evolving? If we go back to history, we find that Charles Dickens had done this for us in the opening paragraph of the novel, *A Tale of Two Cities*, in the context of French Revolution settings.

> It was the best of times, it was the worst of times, it was the age of wisdom, it was the age of foolishness, it was the epoch of belief, it was the epoch of incredulity, it was the season of Light, it was the season of Darkness, it was the spring of hope, it was the winter of despair, we had everything before us, we had nothing before us, we were all going direct to Heaven, we were all going direct the other way.

These memorable lines encapsulate the nuances of our times—the innovations and enrichment in the marketplace of ideas as well as the misery and the poverty of a large majority of people, throughout the world, still in the grip of economic and educational deprivation, to which has been added the Digital Divide.

Digital Divide

The digital divide is not confined to individuals or a section of a society in a country; it is so widespread that it has given rise to concern all over. In a leading article in the *Choices* (June 2000), the UNDP magazine, it was stressed that developing countries must do all they can to bridge an ever more apparent digital divide—the inequities created by differences in ICT availability, access, affordability and capacity. The divide runs between North and South, rich and poor, young and old, literate and illiterate, men and women, and urban and rural dwellers.

Writing in the same issue, the UNDP Administrator Mark Malloch Brown says: In a few short years the Internet has already changed our world beyond all recognition. Everywhere we look, the "dot.com" revolution is transforming the way we live, the way we work, the way we do business. However, he goes on to add,"For many in the developing world and civil society these rapid changes are seen as a threat. Far from helping, the information explosion is seen as a major contributing factor to the growing gap between rich and poor, both within and between countries. As high technology comes to make up an increasingly important part of the global economy, poorer countries with fewer resources and less well-educated workforces are being left further and further behind."

Addressing a conference on, "The challenge of information and communications technology for development," in Tokyo in June 2000, Brown again pointed to the inequities of the whole situation as under:

> ICT is transforming everything it touches, from politics, to business, to culture, to education and to health. And what we have seen is just the tip of an enormous iceberg. But it is an iceberg the developing world is currently at more risk of crashing into than making use of. The information gap is real and growing. Our sister organisation, the International Telecommunications Union, estimates that 96% of Internet host computers reside in high-income countries. There are more hosts in Finland than all of Latin America and more in New York than Africa.

GLOBAL INFORMATION REVOLUTION

One of the challenges confronting the contemporary society is: how to cope with the rapid-fire technological, economic and geopolitical changes; as well as changes in the social and development sector. The term 'change' has in fact become the defining attribute of the closing decades of the twentieth century and we see no let up in this process in the foreseeable future. In this process information has become power. It has the potential to change perceptions, induce paradigm shift in concepts and theories and transform even the well established and stable systems.

In the changed world economy, the sources of higher productivity are increasingly dependent on knowledge and information applied to production, and this knowledge and information is increasingly science-based. Production in the advanced capitalist societies shifts from material goods to information-processing activities, fundamentally changing the structure of these societies.

The new economy is global. Investment, production, management, markets, labour, information and technology are organised across national boundaries. Such economic and organisational transformations are taking place in the backdrop of one of the most significant technological revolutions in the human history.

Information technology and new media have contributed to many of the decentralising and democratic tendencies in the recent past. It has been widely remarked that the electronic media had contributed to the fall of the tyrannical regimes, including the Marcos dictatorship in the Philippines and the communist rule in East Germany and the former Soviet Union. The relentless advance of electronic technology has brought about Information Revolution, the impact of which is still being felt all around in all sections of the society throughout the world. It has been an important contributory factor in encouraging and strengthening the forces of globalisation.

The electronic media, information technology and the news media have converged in a way that has vastly affected the communication system, its operations and working.

Satellite television has created a new cultural market, which transcends national boundaries and has acquired geopolitical significance for this reason. Since satellite television is no respecter of national borders, it has created new electronic communities, which transcend old political boundaries.

Changing News Values

During the closing decades of the twentieth century the media scenario worldwide has undergone complete metamor-phosis. The tools, methods, and formats of news gathering, presentation and analysis have changed. The media consumers—the newspaper readers, radio audience and television viewers have become more discerning and, therefore, more demanding. Today, the newly emerging civil society, which in several cases is taking global dimensions, has a greater share of media cake, and to that extent, the media have been instrumental in strengthening democratic trends in the world at large. At the same time, for the past several years the mainstream media—

leading newspapers, newsmagazines and television—have shown disturbing trends: predominance of kitsch, reducing even serious subjects to frivolity.

It was, of course, premised that with the ongoing trends of globalisation and opening up of economy, the market forces will be a major determining factor in shaping the contours of media. A closer study of the recent trends in media shows that the flippant attitude to matters of serious importance is becoming all too pervasive.

However, a new category of news providers has also emerged on the Internet. They are the *webzines or netzines,* which do not have a print or TV counterpart, but run news service on the Internet. The Internet may not have arrived as a mass medium like television or radio, but it is fast emerging as an influential medium for opinion making. Its reach among non-resident Indians all over the globe is tremendous. But we must realise that unlike other mass media, Internet audiences are different. The Internet reaches people who make a conscious decision to seek information by logging on to a particular site.

Cyber news allows news consumers to understand the meaning of the day's events in a personalised context that makes better sense to them than traditional media do now. Since it can build new communities based on shared interests and concerns and has almost unlimited space to offer levels of repertorial depth, texture and context that are impossible in any other medium-new media can transform journalism.

Another notable feature of the contemporary Global Information Revolution is the emergence of alternate media such as *Al Jazeera, Indymedia* and forum like World Social Forum which represent, by and large, anti-American, anti-globalisation and anti-MNC views so that unheard voices and views also get proper articulation.

Media as Star and Celebrity Journalism

In their book, *War And Anti-War,* Alvin and Heidi Toffler, point out: When we look at the Gulf War, the first in which elements of Third Wave warfare were used decisively; we find that, in a sense, the war may not have been the point of all the media coverage. The media, itself became the 'star' of the spectacle. As former Maj. Gen. Perry Smith, himself a CNN personality noted, 'over the six weeks of the war more people watched more hours of television per day than at any time in history.'

As I am working on the Introduction, sitting in the *Library Learn - UK Online Centre* of the Slough Central Library (June 2004), I find the British press overflowing with several celebrity events:

- The performance of Wayne Rooney in the Euro 2004, which had taken not only UK but the whole of Europe by storm. In its supplement, *The Times,* in its 24 June edition said: It's not just England that Wayne Rooney has taken by storm. The Evertone striker's goalscoring feats in the first group stage of the European Championship have propelled him on to the back– and front – pages of newspapers throughout the world, countries as far afield as Poland and Lebanon. The pictorial feature, Wayne's World: What Planet Earth is making of an England Superstar, carried snapshots from the front pages of newspapers from five countries. Another caption said: A star is born: his four goals so far have made Rooney the hottest property of Euro 2004 and no other youngster has made such an explosive impact since Pelc emerged on the world stage. The just two examples will be insufficient to even imagine the type of hysteria the media had created around Rooney.
- The launching of *My Life* by Bill Clinton was truly on a gigantic scale. Not only the first print order of a record 1.5 million copies, the event had all the trappings of a global media fixture. Mr Clinton kicked off a full throttle publicity campaign to sell his 957-page memoir, which went on sale on 22 June. The launch included high-profile interview with 60 Minutes and *Time* magazine, a lavish book party for a thousand guests in Manhattan and non-stop book signings and television appearances throughout the week.

- The announcement of divorce between Imran Khan and Jemima Goldsmith, after nine years of marriage, gave rise to a number of interviews, articles and features in the British press. *The Times,* in the cover page story in its T2 section of 24 June 2004, carried an interview Burhan Wazir had with Jemima in April 2001, and recalled the history of their marriage, Jemima's life in Pakistan and Imran's life as a politician, along with several photographs.

There are of course, certain subjects for media attention who have gone beyond the status of celebrities and have become icons—such as Diana, John Kennedy and Marilyn Monroe. They continue to fascinate the readers and the media don't seem to have enough of them. Even though after more than five years of the death of Diana in a tragic accident, her memory seems to be fading away, she continues to evoke interest in the media as was evident from the opening of her memorial in the Hyde Park London in July 2004. One of the senior and respected names in the British Journalism, WF Deedes wrote in *The Daily Telegraph* (28 June) about Diana, her strained relations with Charles and latter's relations with Camilla Parker Bowles. Not that these matters have not been written before, but these continue to be of central intreset of the media, in all parts of the world. Here Deedes writes about Diana, as a part of the new collection of essays in his book, *Brief Lives* and says that the princess of Wales was a woman whose gifts were beginning to shine when she died.[1]

An eminent British media academic, James Watson has, while emphasising that if the celebrity does not exist, the 5Ss are the means of achieving it. The 5Ss stand for: Sex, Sensation, Scandal, Sleaze and Soaps.

Interestingly, Anthony Giddens, one of the world's most influential academicians, considers instantaneous electronic communication responsible for creating global celebrities. He says: Instantaneous electronic communication isn't just a way in which news or information is conveyed more quickly. Its existence alters the very texture of our lives, rich and poor alike. When the image of Nelson Mandela may be more familiar to us than the face of our next-door neighbour, something has changed in the nature of our everyday experience. Nelson Mandela is a global celebrity, and celebrity itself is largely a product of new communication technology.

Sensationalism *vs* serious journalism

Since the media in the situation of market economy has to face pressures to cater to the largest segment of readership, it has to take recourse to the standard formula of meeting the requirements of the largest common denominator—the light, and trite and frothy. After the *Daily Mirror* had to fire its editor, Piers Morgan, over the latter's involvement in the infamous episode of printing fake photographs of the British army soldiers brutalising the prisoners in Iraq, his successor, Richard Wallace was selected because he will be concentrating on *froth, fun* and no doubt, *football* (*The Independent* 18 June 2004). *The Times* later commented that paper's sales were hit due to its move towards more serious news. This seems to be the trend worldwide: entertainment or junk journalism, instead of serious and analytical journalism based on independent sources and editorial opinion.

Convergence of media and its complexity

In my quest for literature on the subject I came across a vast treasure of valuable material. One of the most precious is: *A Social History of the Media – from Gutenberg to the Internet* (2002), written by the two British academics Asa Briggs and Peter Burke. A careful reading of the book enriches you with the developments in the media worldwide which few other books would. It quotes the American Markle Foundation Annual Report 1989 which says: Convergence of the media has transformed communications. As new services become widely available, they are changing the ways in which we live and work. It is essential that we understand the effects in order to develop our electronic resources for the benefits of the society.

The last chapter of the book ends with the question mark, Conclusion: Into Cyberspace? And says: The newness in the recent developments in communications, particularly technological, can be greatly exaggerated and that, whatever the coincidences and convergences, there has been no one single line of development. Revealing and useful as it might be to affix labels like, Digital Age, to past and present phenomena, at best they tell us more about perceptions than they do about facts. Their chief characteristic is 'complexity'.

The trends and issues in the contemporary media scenario are indeed complex. They do not offer simplistic analysis and particularly so from the perspective of students and scholars working in the Indian context. However as we go along we attempt to make a tentative but modest effort to understand these complexities.

Human Rights and Media Sensitivity

Human Rights and right to communicate constitutes an integral part of international media landscape. More so with whatever happened to the journalists in the midst of the US attack on Iraq and how the freedom of information got coloured and biased, through 'embedded journalism'. The violation of Human Rights has been greatly focused in the context of the horrific images from Abu Gharib prison in Iraq, of brutalising the prisoners. Leading lights from all over the world led by Desmond Tutu and the British public and political sections have formed Guantanamo Human Rights Commission asking the British Government to investigate reports of abuse and torture of its citizens in Guantanamo.

The reportage created worldwide revulsion in the media against *'the true nature and heart of America'* as *The Guardian* describes in the cover page article of its G2 section of 25 May 2004.

OVERVIEW

The book has been divided into three thematic sections. The first section comprises four chapters· Media Imperialism, Imbalance in International News flow, NWICO and the MacBride Commission Report, Globalisation—a period of historical transition, New Information and Communication Technologies, Multi-media, Satellite Communication, Internet and its Social Impact and New Global Media.

To the developing countries the notion of media imperialism reminds them of the system wherein the rich and powerful media institutions and corporations control information and newsflows, and use these for perpetuating their economic and commercial hold. Such a control naturally leads to imbalance in international newsflows.

As developing countries attained independence, mostly in the later half of the twentieth century, there was all round concern over the degree of penetration by western media. The General Conference of UNESCO, in 1972 drew attention to the way the media of richer countries were a means towards 'the domination of world public opinion or a source of moral and cultural pollution.' Also the dominant First World (North America, Western Europe, Japan and Australia) economies are able to control supply and demand on world markets and poorer countries are encouraged to import First World goods and commodities in exchange for raw materials or cheap labour. The forces of media imperialism also influence the national cultures of the affected countries. Some commentators are of the opinion that the concepts of media imperialism and globalization of culture are linked. The television and mass media programmes of the western countries promote a world wide 'McDonalds and Madonna culture'.

The MacBride Commission compiled a number of statements and opinions from all over the world which recognised the imbalances in information flows. It also cited a statement by the Ministers of Information of the Non-Aligned countreis in New Delhi in July 1976, "The present global information flows are marked by a serious inadequacy and imbalance. The means of communicating information are concentrated in a few countries. The great majority of countries are reduced to being passive recipients of information which is disseminated from a few centres."

The chapter revisits the situation, brought out by media academics as an *afterthought* after 15-20 years. It is noticed that in many ways the situation is not less severe. The global newspower is still heavily Anglo-American.

The New World Information and Communication Order (NWICO) was an effort to give a more balanced view of developing countries than what had been generally presented by the Western press coverage. The establishment of Non-Aligned News Agency (NANA) as a world-wide non-profit making news agency was aimed at achieving greater balance in the reporting of events and developments in the non-aligned countries. However its usefulness has been limited by the competition offered by major news agencies. With the non-aligned movement itself having largely petered out, the Agency has been far from effective.

The constitution of the MacBride Commission, it working and the quality and importance of its report, published as *Many Voices, One World* has also been discussed in the Chapter. The conclusions and recommendations of the Commission have been given as an Annexure.

The chapter on globalisation discusses the impact of the phenomenon on political, economic, cultural and social aspects of the contemporary society. Interestingly, the pace of globalisation is so fast that during the last 3-4 years the term globalisation itself has become more globalised. At the same time anti-globalisation moment has also been taking shape in several parts of the world. The proponents of the movement say that the global information revolution is directed by media corporations like CNN and Disney who treat their audience as consumers not only in goods, but also in ideas, philosophies and ideologies.

The cultural dimensions of globalisation, the advertising practices of MNCs and impact of television programmes over audiences world wide, ushering in of a consumer society are discussed.

The factors accelerating the pace of globalisation are technology, television and travel. Technology has been instrumental in evolving new organizations and work culture.

Globalisation has also led to the creation of 24-hour society. Portability of electronic communication technologies has led to the growth of teleworking. It has given rise to intense competition in service sectors – banking, software management, journalism and trade. An awareness of the trends in globalisation and its impact on society is absolutely essential to the understanding how our life style and living are changing. All these changes are intimately associated with the media technologies, as Professor Giddens explains in the Reith Lectures.

During the 1980, the New Information and Communication Technologies (NICTs) transformed the world of media. Newspapers began to be edited and printed from several centres at the same time, all in different towns and even in different countries – allowing for simultaneous editions of the same newspaper catering to several major areas. Multiplication of television channels, cable television, satellite broadcasting dramatically expanded the territory and expanse of broadcasting.

Within a space of few years, these developments in global media have been joined by an even more revolutionary technology – Internet, which has given rise to new ideology – *Internetphilia.* Some observers of the contemporary society have gone to the extent of saying that Internet is not just a new way to communicate, it is a market place where they can put orders out for bids, it is an instant newspaper for its staff, it is an ever order facility for its customers plus an endlessly updates inventory of those customers likings and dislikings. Internet has suddenly accelerated the pace of change but at the same time it has given rise to serious concern on several social aspects because of its misuse for questionable purposes. Internet has been used to create "hate sites", on-line child pornography, child abuse and "grooming of children". Chatrooms are particularly popular with children and teenagers and there is a risk that paedophiles or sex abusers might use them for victims.

Search engines – the market makers of the Internet – connect consumers with providers at the very moment of consumer interest and enable all of us to find what we want, when we want it. In the intensely competitive world of search engines, better means higher, and higher means a much greater probability that an individual will click on your link.

There is no doubt that NICTs, satellite communication and Internet have suddenly opened up our whole world and we are confronted with a wider and more extensive choices for putting across our point of view. In fact we are living in an era of, "wider, more open and more extensive forms of media in our working and social worlds." Its consequences are still emerging—but one thing is certain—it has been instrumental in globalising our economy and trade and has also led to cultural homogenization.

The fifth chapter discusses the new global media, international media institutions, news agencies and alternate media organisations. Some of the international media institutions like BBC, Reuters, CNN have become truly global information multi-nationals, disseminating news worldwide on 24-hour basis. These organisations—some say—media giants, media conglomerates or media multi-nationals–have changed the rules of games as few things have in recent history.

Some of these institutions like BBC and Reuters have established their prestige and position which remain unchallenged; others have made valuable contribution to the craft of journalism. Even a brief introduction to the international news agencies gives us an idea of the vastness of the task of disseminating the news and bringing it to the door steps of the readers.

The chapter on Intellectual Property Rights discusses concepts like copyright, patent, trade mark and design. The section on Guidance for the Students will be particularly useful for the students because they would know how to use copyright material for their research work. Of particular significance for the students in India is the section on TRIPs agreement—an understanding of which is essential in the context of developing countries. The way successful attempts have been made in the past to register patents even on traditional Indian crops and tree (*neem*) shows that developing countries have a long battle ahead in order to protect their interests. I am glad the UGC Curriculum Development Committee thought it fit to include this topic, which will create greater awareness amongst the students and faculty on the seriousness of the issues involved.

Similarly other topics such as Universal Declaration of Human Rights and the Right to Communication, help develop a broad perspective on issues of contemporary relevance. The Human Development Report (2000) stresses that media can mobilise public opinion by spreading awareness of human rights policies and highlighting violations. In many countries media are a major force for reporting and demanding accountability. Cyber networks have brought attention to rights, disseminating information on good practices and on violation of rights. Educating policy makers, the army and police about human rights is essential for creating a human rights culture. The media, in a way, have brilliantly succeeded in highlighting the excesses committed by the US forces on the prisoners and the public of Iraq. There is an imperative danger that presently USA is in the mode of acting like an imperial power of the 21st century. It has, in any case become the super-cop of the world. Whereas it is essential to fight the evil forces fueling terrorism, but to invade countries in search of non existing WMDs smacks of arrogance and a patently dangerous portent for world peace.

The concluding chapter underlines India's position in the Global Information Revolution. Needless to say that it is not easy to formulate an easy, facile construction for a country of India's vastness and dimensions. In India bullock carts and cyber marts would continue to exist side by side. In a way both the aspects depict the two trends—traditional and rural ethos alongside the modern and global mindset of information technology settings. As the chapter clearly underlines, in India one can observe a unique communication experience—oral and traditional, face-to-face communication in vast congregations of people disseminated and magnified through vast infrastructure of electronic media.

However the rapid progress that India has made in IT industry has helped transform its image as an engine of growth and an economic powerhouse. During the recent years India has witnessed an exponential growth in Cable TV, Cyber Cafes and IT training institutes. E-governance is also making headway-rather slowly.

Finally, how does one see the broad trends in international communication. Two examples will illustrate these trends:

The Advertising giant *Saatchi & Saatchi*, in one of their annual reports refer to the modern world as one giant market of products and brand names as under :

> We live in an era of Global communication. Scientists and technologists have achieved what militarists and statesmen down the ages have attempted to establish but without success – the global empire. There is no doubt that the world is becoming one market place. Capital markets, products and services, management and manufacturing techniques have all become global in nature. As a result, companies increasingly find that they must compete all over the world-in the global market place. This new development is emerging at the same time as advanced technology is transforming information and communication.
>
> – Cited in *Global Television An Introduction*

Another example is from an ancient institution – a respected member of the *Fourth Estate – The Times*, which became such a force that for a long time it was considered to be the fourth estate itself. One of the editors of the *Sunday Times*, Harold Evans, wrote a book *Good Times, Bad Times*, which encapsulates all that is good and great in journalism, and who won great victories for the freedom of the press. *The Times*, which started life as *The Daily Universal Register* in 1785 and changed title three years later to *The Times*, brought out a bicentenary volume in which the Editor, Charles Douglas-Home wrote :

> The electronic age will spawn many ancillary publishing enterprises to support newspapers. These will penetrate new markets which might only want a fraction of what we offer every day in our pages for the general reader. They should not, however, so preoccupy us that they lift our attention from the main aim, which is to produce an excellent paper every day, much as our predecessors have done for the past 200 years.

> Thus at the start of every day and at the end, it is the newspaper coming through the letter box, unfolding on the breakfast table, and embracing a constituency of readership which has some sense of community about it and some almost subliminal connection with the writers and editors on the paper's staff, which is the living organism. Were it not for that, I do not believe that any newspaper would have survived 200 years. It is because of that that I expect our paper to survive the next 200 years.

I would go in—any day, for an ancient institution like *The Times,* which to me represents stability, and a journey into the world of ideas, rather than the fiz and froth of market place—represented by its most famous global brand name—Coca Cola.

Pick you choose. That is the freedom that international communication offers.

NOTE

In its issue of 17 September 2004, *The Daily Telegraphy,* carries an interview of Harry on Diana, in which Prince Harry is scathing of those sections of media whose interest in her is largely salacious. Prince Harry vents his frustration at former royal aids and confidants who have sold intimate details about Diana.

REFERENCES

Giddens, Anthony (2000). *Runaway World,* Profile Books, London.

Singhal, Arvind and Rogers, Everett M. (2001) *India's Communication Revolution,* Sage Publication, New Delhi.

UNDP (2000) Human Development Report, *Human Rights and Human Development,* Oxford University Press.

UNESCO (1982) *Many Voices, One World,* Report of the International Commission on the Study of Communication Problems, Paris.

World Bank (2000) *World Development Report 1999-2000. Entering the 21st Century.* Oxford University Press.

2

MEDIA IMPERIALISM, IMBALANCE IN INTERNATIONAL NEWS FLOW

NWICO and MacBride Commission Reprot

In the 1970s, international debates on communication problems centred around issues like media imperialism, imblanace in international newsflow, and concentration and monopolies in the communication industry. These issues were stridently discussed and reached points of confrontation in many areas. Whereas the Third World countries protested against the dominant flow of news from the industrialised countries; their contentions were countered as attacks on free flow of information. There were differences on subjects like news values, rights and responsibilities of journalists and the contribution of mass media to national development.

The United Nations Educational, Scientific and Cultural Organization (UNESCO), the lead agency in the UN system became the forum for articulating views on these issues. Therefore the General Conference of UNESCO in its nineteenth session, held at Nairobi in 1976 decided "that highest priority should be given to measures aiming at reducing communication gap existing between developed and developing countries and at achieving a freer and more balanced international flow of information", and that "a review should be undertaken of the totality of the problems of communication in modern society."

The Director General of UNESCO, Amadou Mahtar M'Bow therefore appointed a 16-member commission—International Commission for the Study of Communication Problems, under the chairmanship of Sean MacBride, holder of Nobel and Lenin Peace Prizes, journalist and former Minister of Foreign Affairs, Ireland. The members of the commission were drawn from different political, economic and geographical spectrum from all over the world and included journalists and broadcasters, researchers and academics, organisational heads of news agencies and press foundations. A senior and respected journalist and former editor of *The Hindustan Times,* B.G. Verghese represented India. The Report of the Commission—*Many Voices, One World; Communication and Society – Today and Tomorrow* constitutes one of the most precious documents in the field of communication studies. For the present author, the report remains one of the most valuable resources for his study and writing work.

This chapter will discuss issues such as media imperialism, NWICO, NAMEDIA conference in New Delhi, IPDC and contents of the MacBride Commission report. The Conclusions and Recommendations of the Report have been given in the Annexure.

All in all it appears that the issues raised and debated in the 1980s are as relevant today as they were at that time.

MEDIA IMPERIALISM

The issue of media imperialism resonates with the old phenomenon of colonialism; except that it is more pervasive today; its nature and scope has changed. Media imperialism has various manifestations; monopolization of media, concentration of media industries or domination or control of Third World and developing countries media by the capitalist, western media. Surprisingly, literature on the subject originating from the western countries is quite critical of the phenomenon. The best way to understand the issue is to refer to the opinions expressed by leading authors and commentators over a period of time, starting from the MacBride Commission report which says: We can sum up by stating that in the communication industry there is a relatively small number of predominant corporations which integrate all aspects of production and distribution, which are based in the leading developed countreis and which have become transnational in their operations. Concentration of resources and infrastructures is not only a growing trend, but also a worrying phenomenon which may adversely affect the freedom and democratization of communication. Concentration and transnationalization are the consequences, perhaps inevitable of the interdependence of various technologies and various media, the high costs of research and development and the ability of the most powerful firms to penetrate any market.

The observations of the commission have been rather cautious; not so comments by other authors who see such concentration as a process historically linked to the more general economic and political processes of first colonial, and then imperial, developments in the twentieth century. This is elaborated by authors Tim O'Sullivan and others in their book, *Studying the Media* as under :

'Imperialism' in this sense refers to the ways in which certain industrialised nation states have emerged as *world powers,* by extending their forms of control and rule over other political, economic and cultural communities and nations for the purposes of commercial advantage, military security, political or ideological 'mission', etc. Whereas colonialism is viewed as an early stage in this process, predominantly concerned with economic advantage and exploitation, imperialism results from wider and more complex forms of dominance, directed towards empire building at the global level. Imperialism is the systematic production of massive disparities in wealth, power and influence, on a worldwide scale. Dominant, 'First World' (a term usually referring to North America, Western Europe, Japan and Australia) economies are able to control supply and demand on world markets, and poorer countries are encouraged to import First World goods and commodities in exchange for raw materials or cheap labour. (p. 288)

Another author, David McQueen, in his book, *Television : A Media Student's Guide* cites a Canadian writer Don Rojas who gives a clear picture of the phenomenon called *information imperialism* (pp 241-42). The text is reproduced as under :—

INFORMATION IMPERIALISM

Ninety per cent of international news published by the world's press comes from the 'big four' Western news agencies. They are United Press International (UPI), Associated Press (AP), Reuter and Agence France Presse (AFP). Two are American, one is British, one is French. Their output is supplemented by the transnational giants: from Murdoch to Times Warner to CNN. Almost all of these are American. The largest news agency, UPI, gets 80 per cent of its funding from US newspapers. A survey in the mid-1980s found that UPI devoted 71 per cent of its coverage to the United States, 9.6 per cent to Europe, 5.9 per cent to Asia, 3.2 per cent to Latin America, 3 per cent to the Middle East and 1.8 per cent to Africa.

'These figures', wrote the Canadian writer Don Rojas in *Third World Resurgence,* 'give a clear picture of *the phenomenon called information imperialism.* In the total volume of UPI's information, news about the United States took up more space than that devoted to the whole African continent, where more than 50 countries are situated.' Former Tanzanian President Julius Nyerere once noted sarcastically, wrote Rojas, that the inhabitants of developing countries should be allowed to take part in the presidential elections of the United States because they are bombarded with as much information about the candidates as are North American citizens (*Third World Resurgence,* issue 12, quoted in Pilger, 1992).

However the latest take from the book: *One No, Many Yeses* is most instructive. The book discusses the phenomenon of anti-globalisation world wide and the author Paul Kingsnorth quotes the discussion with one of America's most respected, and most uncompromising media critics David Barsamian, who is also the founder and Director of Alternative Radio, whose programmes are now featured on 125 stations. He says: Look at the big picture. Look at what has happened to American journalism. Ben Bagdikian's classic book, *The Media Monopoly* has always been the primer for what is happening to our media. It came out in 1983, and in it he identified fifty corporations that controlled most of the media in the United

States. Second edition came out—twenty-eight. Third edition—twenty-three. Fourth edition—fourteen. Fifth edition—ten. The latest edition, which came out in 2000, identified six corporations. And these corporations are now subsumed in even bigger corporations. CNN and ABC are controlled by Disney. NBC is controlled by General Electric. These are no longer news gathering organisations in control of their own destiny. They are controlled by entertainment companies interested in maximising profits... This concentration of monopoly control of information poses a *serious* (italics in the original) threat to democracy.

The most worrying aspect is that forces of media imperialism, media monopoly/media concentration are stronger, entrenched as ever, all protests notwithstanding. They influence the national culture of the affected countries.

Although the situation in developing countries is changing fast and television is no longer confined to metropolitan areas, even then it has given rise to the class of people whose tastes, aspirations, fashions and life styles are more Westernised than others in the society.

The development of global communication technologies has been in consonance with the requirements of capitalism for new markets. According to McQueen :—

> The threat to independence in the late twentieth century from the new electronics could be greater than was colonialism itself.... The new media have the power to penetrate more deeply into a 'receiving' culture than any other previous manifestation of Western technology. The results could be immense havoc, an intensification of the social contradictions within developing societies today (Smith, 1980).

In effect the concepts of 'media imperialism' and the 'globalization of culture' are inextricably linked. *Global communications are owned and controlled, almost exclusively, by 'First World' (US, European, Australian and Japanese) corporate interests and largely by a handful of US transnational conglomerates.*

In this sense *a worldwide 'McDonalds and Madonna'* culture, *as promoted by television and the mass media, is seen as powerful and threatening to local identity, creating economic dependence, social pacification and cultural displacement.*

Imbalance in International Newsflow

The MacBride Commission made a comprehensive study of the issue in Part III of the Report: Problems and Issues of Common Concern. Chapter I – Flaws in Communication Flows, cites a number of studies, opinions and examples throughout the discussion. The sources and the range of opinions are most diverse. Only one such statement from the lengthy footnote on page 142 will be sufficient to indicate the problem. It says: Recognition of existing imbalances in information flows between unequal partners is no longer a controversial issue. From various view points and sources, the fact is admitted; the following are typical statements by *Le Monde Diplomatique,* the sharing out of this power (information) which is monopolized in national societies by the dominant classes and elites or the established powers, and at the international level by governments and private transnational corporations, a few news agencies and publishing companies or telecommunication and data processing industries in industrialised countries – which ensure a one-way flow of information to developing countries (January 1979, Paris).

During the intervening twenty-five years there have been changes in the way information flows. There have been more community radio stations where participation at the programme production is more democratic, regional language press which brings out more news from districts and rural areas and the Internet which is providing an alternate source of information dissemination. Some of these alternate sources are discussed elsewhere in the book, but by and large the big picture remains the same.

In the wake of the UNESCO debate about the proposed New World Information and Communication Order (NWICO), several news agencies and news exchange mechanisms (NEMs) were formed throughout the developing world. Some of these were: Inter Press Service (IPS), Non-aligned News Agencies Pool (NANAP), the Pan-African News Agency (PANA), and the Caribbean News Agency (CANA). Except for the IPS, most of these have been interagency co-operative ventures sponsored by the governments. On behalf of UNESCO, a study of these organisations was conducted by Boyd-Barrett and Thussu. Their conclusion was :

NEMs do not appear to have had a significant impact on the structures of media imperialism over the past two decades. The development and maintenance of local and regional centres of news exchange does not in and of itself indicate a weakening in the global market hold of the major western transnationals.

The Asian Mass Communication Research and Information Centre (AMIC) Singapore in 1996, brought out a publication: *Opening Windows – Issues in Communication,* which was essentially a selection of articles published in *Media Asia,* AMIC's quarterly journal which commenced publication in 1974. This Silver Jubilee Collection contains an article by Boyd-Barrett: New Perspectives, New Directions, published in *Media Asia* in Vol. 8, No. 4 (1981). The article was written when the NWICO debate was still at the height of its influence. The author added an *Afterthought* to the article—which gives author's views after a period of 15 years. In the *Afterthought* the author says:

In many ways the situation today is no less severe. There are some significant changes, but it is easy to be misled into thinking that these changes have profoundly altered the underlying dynamics of power and influence in global news media. The most outstanding development since 1981 has been the growth of the television or video news agencies and the demise which they represent between "wholesale" and "retail" distinctions in the markets served by these agencies. Two of these agencies, Reuters Television and APTV, have connections with the old "Big 4" print agencies. Another, WTN, grew out of the old UPITN. There are some important newcomers—notably, CNN—and some old players are no longer so influential—notably UPI. The relative ranking of different agencies has also undergone some surprising developments: in 1981, it would still have been difficult to predict just how enormously successful would be the future of Reuters' involvement in financial and economic news services, even though the most important measures (other than stock market flotation) were already underway at that time. In 1981 nobody could have predicted the collapse so soon of the Soviet Union and the eastern communist block. This has brought about a reconfiguration of agency influence in what was once termed the "Second World", and has also seen the emergence of a late generation of new national news agencies.

Despite the changes, however, *global news power is still heavily Anglo-American.*

If anything, the American influence as the global news power has increased, alternative news sources and news agencies notwithstanding.

In the same publication, Bella Mody, a well known communication researcher says that technology options for Third World countries are limited by our financial capital constraints and by technical underdevelopment. Pointing to the difficulties encountered in raising funds for communication projects Mody says, "The bilateral nature and the low level of US financial contributions to the UNESCO IPDC, an organisation originally proposed by the US, bears witness to the donor's partisan interests. The fact is that the donors (now withholders) of big sums of aid are, for the most part, the old colonial powers that continue to influence their one-time colonies through their transnational corporations." The perception in the article, written in 1984, regarding transnational corporations influencing the economic and socio-cultural policies of the host countries, has, if any, strengthened further during the course of 20 years.

Media imperialism continues to operate in the world because of the high cost of broadcasting, specially as Western markets have large advertising revenues and can afford to dump their programmes and films on developing nations.

NEW WORLD INFORMATION AND COMMUNICATION ORDER (NWICO)

At the fourth summit of the non-aligned countries in Algiers in September 1973, a programme of action was adopted which encouraged member states to work for the, "reorganisation" of existing communication channels, which are the legacy of the colonial past and which have hampered free, direct and fast communication between them." The programme proposed revision of cable tarrifs, agreements on joint use of, and guidelines for communication satellites, and increased contact and exchange of experience between the media institutions in the non-aligned countries.

Subsequently, the symposium on mass media in the non-aligned countries in March 1976 endorsed the programme. It was in the report of this symposium that the NWICO concept was used for the first time.

At a conference of ministers from the non-aligned counties held in New Delhi in July 1976, the concept was developed further. The declaration adopted at the Conference stated that the present global flow of information was characterised by serious deficiencies and inequalities.... In a situation in which the means of information are dominated and monopolized by a few agencies to spread information as they wish, at the same time the rest are denied the right to inform and be informed objectively and accurately. The declaration stated that the major international news agencies had ignored or distorted the foreign policy efforts of non-aligned nations and that these nations had few possibilities of getting to know about each other through other channels.

This new concept was mentioned for the first time in a UN resolution at the 33rd session of the General Assembly in 1978. The resolution included a paragraph on the need of establishing a new information and communication order in the world.

NAMEDIA Conference in New Delhi

An interesting debate on the new order took place at the non-aligned conference on the media—NAMEDIA—which was held in New Delhi in December 1983. This meeting was attended by practising journalists, media researchers and information authorities from the non-aligned countries. It was for the first time practising press professionals from these countries were actively drawn into the discussion on the contents of the demands for a new information and communication order.

The NAMEDIA debate produced concrete and radically new points of view. The resolutions from the conference stressed the fact that developing countries must create their own communication technology, suited to local needs and economic possibilities. An important requirement for this technology is that it can be made available to the local community and engage local resources.

For the first time, feminist perspectives were included in a non-aligned resolution on the new order. An active group of women at the conference proposed a text which stated that the new order would be just as much a distortion as the old one unless all oppressed groups—and particularly women—were granted full access to the media. The male majority was not willing to go that far. But the women were responsible for the inclusion in the resolution of unambiguous demands for the participation of both sexes in communication and for the presentation by the media of a realistic picture of the conditions determining the lives of women. Thus they contributed to adding a new and significant dimension to the concept of a new information and communication order.

The participants at the conference in New Delhi did not limit themselves to criticizing the Western media, but also underlook a critical evaluation of media practices within the non-aligned countries. Attention was directed to the obstacles which inhibit the flow of information within the countries of the Third World. The declaration adopted by NAMEDIA stated that media professionals in the non-aligned countries were not only engaged in surmounting international inequalities but also strived to extend the domain of freedom in their own countries (NAMEDIA, 1983). This is an illustration of the fact that the call for a new information order contained possibilities for freeing creative forces.

It was at twenty-first session of General Conference in Belgrade in 1980 that the UNESCO began to work earnestly on the content of the new concept. The MacBride Commission had already established the frame work.

While elaborating the concept, the General Conference, in paragraph 14, stated the considerations on which the NWICO could be based :—

(a) (i) elimination of the imbalances and inequalities which characterize the present situation;

(ii) elimination of the negative effects of certain monopolies, public or private, and excessive concentrations;

(iii) Removal of the internal and external obstacles to a free flow and wider and better balanced dissemination of information and ideas;

(iv) plurality of sources and channels of information;

(v) freedom of the press and information;

(vi) the freedom of journalists and all professionals in the communication media, a freedom inseparable from responsibility;

(vii) the capacity of developing countries to achieve improvement of their own situations, notably by providing their own equipment, by training their personnel, by improving their infrastructures and by making their information and communication media suitable to their needs and aspirations;

(viii) the sincere will of developed countreis to help them attain these objectives;

(ix) respect for each people's cultural identity and for the right of each nation to inform the world public about its interests, its aspirations and its social and cultural values;

(x) respect for the right of all peoples to participate in international exchanges of information on the basis of equality, justice and mutual benefit; and

(xi) respect for the right of the public, of ethnic and social groups and of individuals to have access to information sources and to participate actively in the communication process;

(b) this new world information and communication order should be based on the fundamental principles of international law, as laid down in the Charter of the United Nations;

(c) diverse solutions to information and communication problems are required because social, political, cultural and economic problems differ from one country to another, and within a given country, from one group to another.

International Programme for Development of Communication (IPDC)

An American initiative at the twentieth session of the General Conference UNESCO in 1978 provided impetus for the establishment of IPDC. The leader of the American delegation stated that if the countries of the world were not be divided into two camps for ever—the information rich and the information poor—it would be necessary to organize systematic, long range and concerted international cooperation for communication development.

In the basic texts of UNESCO General Conference, the objectives of the IPDC, divided into four main categories are as under :—

Assistance

The IPDC is to assist developing countries, at their request, with analysis of their communication needs and with planning and development of their capacity in the field of communication, in particular concerning the contribution of communication to endogenous economic, social and cultural development. The IPDC is also to promote reciprocal consultations among institutions in the developing countries.

Co-ordination

The IPDC is to strengthen co-operation and co-ordination among all the parties which are engaged in international communication development, both within and outside the UN system. The IPDC is also to encourage contact between those who require assistance and those who can offer the needed assistance.

Information

The IPDC is to gather information on global needs and resources, study the experience which is gained on international co-operation in the field of communication development, and contribute to increased awareness as to the significance of communication for the development process.

Financing

The IPDC is to seek to encourage contributions to communication projects from all available sources and to mobilize the resources which are needed to carry out the first three tasks.

The four objectives encompassed essentially everything which touched on international communication development. For this reason, one of the first challenges facing the IPDC Council was to decide on a realistic limitation of their responsibilities. The main emphasis was placed on increasing the capacity to use those means of communication which were available to poor countries at a reasonable price. But experience has shown that in this field as well, priorities must be established and criteria drawn up to strengthen activities which truly benefit the groups which are in greatest need of increased opportunities for communication.

At their second meeting, in January 1982, the IPDC Council decided to give priority to eight different areas of activity as far as approving and financing projects was concerned. Some of these areas were: planning and research in those countries which had the least developed communication systems; basic investments necessary for producing, storing, disseminating and receiving information, with main emphasis on the development of endogenous technology and expertise, development of media infrastructures, training of media professionals in all areas of communication, reciprocal co-operation among developing countreis, and the use of communication to promote development in other areas, such as education, agriculture, health services and rural development.

The IPDC inspired high expectations of promoting practical results. Much of the reason for establishing the programme was precisely the wish to get away from ideological debate and into a situation with increasing emphasis on cooperative efforts for the concrete development of basic communication in the poorest countries. At the same time there were those who still doubted whether IPDC would in fact be able to shoulder this task. They feared that political disputes on information issues would crop up again in the new institution as well. For this reason it was important for the IPDC to get started on a practical working programme.

[Based on UNESCO documents on *Communication and Society*—15—by Gunnar Garbo]

MacBride Commission Report

The report of the commission titled as—*Many Voices, One World,* was the outcome of the hard work and deliberations of the "brains trust" (as Secretary General M'Bow says in his Foreword to the report) composed of highly competent, prominent figures drawn from various background. Apart from the meetings held at the UNESCO headquarters in Paris, a large number of seminars and consultations were organised during the tenure of the commission. The Commission also had the benefit of hundreds of individual, institutional and governmental comments on the Interim Report of the Commission submitted in 1978.

The President of Commission, Sean MacBride in his Preface says; "While our report represents the Commission's collective vision of the communication scene it has been based on a virtually worldwide survey of opinions, both individual and institutional, and a mountain of documentation from myriad sources. This wealth of information covered the widest possible spectrum of ideological, political, socio-economic and cultural colourings."

The Report indeed makes a very wide survey of almost all the issues associated with communication. It discusses the historical, contemporary and international dimensions of the issues. It also discusses means, infrastructures and concentrations and transnationalization of communication industry. Part III of Problems and Issues of Common Concern deal with topics like market dominance, cultural alienation, violation of human rights and equal rights of women and discusses communication policies, research contributions and rights and responsibilities of journalists.

Equally important are general comments given by some of the members individually and Notes on Definitions, International Satellite Systems and the list of International Organizations active in various communication fields.

There is absolutely no doubt that Report presents a comprehensive, inclusive, analytical study of all issues concerning communication and society. Most of its conclusions and recommendations are as valid today as at the time when these were made. The Commission laid the framework for NWICO and IPDC. It is a different matter that some of the western countries, particularly USA and UK thought it fit to withdraw from UNESCO itself [The USA returned to UNESCO only in 2004]. Some of problems—particularly those of control and domination of media institutions and infrastructure by MNCs and the western countries—continue unabated.

REFERENCES

Asian Media Information and Communication Centre (1996), *Opening Windows : Issues in Communication,* Singapore.

David McQueen (1998), *Television : A Media Student's Guide,* Arnold, London.

Gunnar Garbo : *A World of Difference : The International Distribution of Information : The Media and Developing Countries,* UNESCO Paris.

Paul Kingsnorth (2003), *One No, Many Yeses : A Journey to the Heart of Global Resistance Movement,* Simon and Schuster, UK Ltd. London.

Tim O Sullivan, Brian Dutton, Philip Rayner (1998), *Studying the Media,* Arnold, London.

UNESCO (1982), *Many Voices, One World,* Report of the International Commission on the Study of Communication Problems, Paris.

3

GLOBALISATION

A Period of Historical Transition

> There are good reasons to believe that we are living through a major period of historical transition. The changes affecting us are not confined to any one area of globe but stretch almost everywhere.
>
> Anthony Giddens – Director, London School of Economics
> In Introduction to
> *Runaway World, How Globalisation is reshaping our lives.*

The above excerpt, taken from the BBC Reith lectures* for the year 1999, by and large, sums up the spirit of globalisation.

Globalisation is the keyword which underlines the temper of contemporary society. There is hardly any aspect which remains untouched by the impact of globalisation. All issues whether economic, political, cultural and technological have been impacted by this phenomenon, and in turn, have also been responsible for accelerating and deepening the phenomenon.

---

* *Reith Lectures:* The Reith Lectures are a series of annual radio lectures given by leading figures of the day, and broadcast by the BBC. They were begun in 1948, in honour of the first Director-General of the BBC, John Reith.

In 1948, Bertrand Russell spoke on 'Authority and the Individual'. The well known historian and philosopher, Arnold Toynbee, in 1952 spoke on 'The World and the West'. In 1966, the eminent economist and former US ambassador to India, J. K. Galbraith spoke on 'The New Industrial State'. In 2003, Vilayanur S. Ramachandran spoke on 'The Emerging Mind'. The 2004 Reith Lecture by Nobel Prize-winning poet and playwright, Wole Soyinka was on 'Climate of Fear'.

The five lectures by Anthony Giddens, who is Britain's leading contemporary social thinker, were marked by a further new departure because these were the first given internationally; London, Hong Kong, Delhi and Washington. The lectures initiated, what the eminent speaker says in the preface to the above book, *An Electronic Global Conversation about Globalisation.* The lectures not only provoked vigorous response from the audiences, but also succeeded in building around these lectures an Internet debate.

Interestingly, in the second edition of the book brought out in May 2002, Giddens revisits the ongoing phenomenon in the preface, which substantively takes note of the events occurring after 11 September, 2001. In the opening paragraphs of the preface he makes two important points; that the term globalisation has itself become more *globalised* and that since late 1998, when the talks were being written anti-globalisation movement has set in giving rise to protests and demonstrations worldwide.

Globalisation is integrated with the development of information technology that is radically altering the world's economic boundaries. It is not only that the offices on two continents can communicate as if they were on the same street; it is the effect that information technology is having on labour migration. Developing countries, once viewed as the sources of raw material are now seen as possible locations for inexpensive labour. Multinationals are creating an increasing number of low-paying jobs in developing countries. Television, technology and travel are considered as the main factors responsible for accelerating the pace of globalisation.

Globalisation has led to the development of global pop culture. Coca-Cola is sold in more countries than the United Nations has members and it is claimed that 'Coke' is second most universally understood term in English after 'Okay'. Levis jeans are sold in more than seventy countries. German game shows and Brazilian soap opera are popular on Cameroon television. International students from Kenya are relieved to discover that Kentucky Fried chicken is available in the United

States too. And Wal-Mart stores in Mexico display signs stating 'Proudly Mexican'. (*Intercultural Communication,* p 327)

There are a number of aspects of globalisation - economic, social, technological and cultural - that it would be in order to present some of the key statements. This will enable us to put the pieces together in a possible attempt to make a sense of the whole.

The Australian sociologist, Malcolm Waters argues that in a single global society and culture, territoriality will disappear as an organising principle for social and cultural life. He sees flows of goods, people and ideas linking together previously homogenous cultural niches forcing each other to 'revitalise' itself to others. He defines revitalising as to compare, contrast and position. From this position, Waters defines globalisation as:

> A social process in which the constraints of geography on economic, social and cultural arrangements recede, in which people become increasingly aware that they are receding and in which people act accordingly.

In the introduction to *Runaway World,* Giddens says: In a globalising world, where information and images are routinely transmitted across the globe, we are all regularly in contact with others who think differently, and live differently from ourselves. Cosmopolitans welcome and embrace this cultural complexity. Fundamentalists find it dangerous and disturbing.

In the book, *One No, Many Yeses,* Paul Kingsnorth says: We are in the midst of a global information revolution which is leading not, as its proponents claim, to more 'choice', better quality media and more perspectives on the world, but to an ever-contracting group of earth-encircling corporations mediating the stories that shape our world. We become consumers not just in goods, but in ideas, philosophies, and ideologies. They entertain us, we sit and listen - but not until we've paid them. Stories have always defined the way societies and culture sees them. Now the lens through which we view the world is owned by CNN and fairy tales are told by Disney, which merchandise tie-ins at Burger King.

Writing in *Virtual States: The Internet and the Boundaries of the Nation-State*, Jerry Everard* says: Among the process of change being brought about by globalisation and the advent of global communications is the change in the face of the politics. When demonstrators in Russia and Albania hold up placards and banners written in English, it is clear that electronic media and the adoption of English as the lingua franca of the electronic media has rewritten the nature of political life at a global level (p 51) and, "The increasingly global spread of Internet is set to bring changes at least as great as shift from print to radio and television. Perhaps it will bring a philosophically more important change: from an economy of objects to an economy of signs, and from a philosophical world of nouns, to one of verbs. Already the distinctions are blurring within language, as verbs become nominalised, and nouns are transformed into verbs. We 'e-mail' each other, 'satellite-in' the news, become 'informationalised' or 'network'" (p156).

Some other elucidations on the subject include: the UN Secretary General Kofi Annan takes globalisation as 'world inclusivity', and of-course, for Microsoft Moghul Bill Gates it could not be anything other than 'the world united by the Web'.

Since the concept of globalisation has caught the academic and intellectual circles variously, there are bound to be a wider range of opinions and points of views on the subject.

GLOBALISATION AND CULTURAL CHANGE

The cultural dimension of globalisation has come in for extensive comments and serious concern in the writings of sociologists and scholars of media studies. The trading and advertising practices of MNCs and impact of television programmes over audiences worldwide, leading to homogeneity of culture has been a recurrent theme in such writings. The domination of MNC-controlled media and their profit making propensity, the role of transnational advertising

---

* The author is in the department of English and Theatre studies at the Australian National University.

agencies in ushering in a consumer society have been some of the main causes for setting in of anti-globalisation movement throughout the world. Intrinsic to the issues of globalisation and cultural change is the notion of cultural imperialism. Some writers have pointed out that globalisation ultimately leads to homogeneity on an increasingly worldwide basis.

They also say the word 'media' has become relay stations for the most powerful multinational corporations and their forms of popular, profitable culture.

Those in the anti-globalisation movement say that *'Manufactured Culture'* is replacing real culture and consider the American consumption patterns responsible for spreading western consumerism. They say that western consumerism has broken through the geographical boundaries and is spreading itself all over the map.

The domination of western culture values, consumption patterns and the way MNCs are instrumental in strengthening the process, as well as commercialisation of media, all point towards leading the whole world towards Western cultural hegemony abetted by the multi-national media corporations, which are increasingly converting themselves into multinational entertainment corporations. In this context Kingsnorth says 'The outcome of allowing key sources of nation's information, news and cultural expression to be controlled by an ever narrowing cabal of giant profit-making entertainment corporations can be seen any time a television set is switched on in America. The attitude of Disney's chief executive, Michael Eisner sums up the issue as well as any activist could, when he explains his company's mission, 'We have no obligation to make history, we have no obligation to make art, we have no obligation to make a statement. To make money is our only objective'. It is, therefore, imperative that inexorable forces of globalisation are ushering in and strengthening the trends towards making more money and, therefore, market forces are swaying the economic and social policies all over the world. Those who are not a part of market economy are doomed to remain on the margins of the society.

GLOBALISATION AND 24-HOUR SOCIETY

The pace of change is so fast that we have begun to live in what many sociologists, and writers on contemporary social trends, call as 24-hour society. Technology has not only accelerated the process of globalisation but it has also been instrumental in evolving new organisations and new work culture, absolutely different from what we have been used to so far. The nature of employment is changing all over the world. The stability of employment, with features like retirement and pension, is disappearing and more and more of us are becoming 'portfolio workers'. These portfolio workers generally hop from one organisation to another or, from one department of the same organisation to another quite often, and they have to pick up the nature of the job so fast that life and living is becoming more and more stressful. Since most organisations, in the present phase of competition, resort to cost-cutting and downsizing, employees have to face up to the ever new challenges that the changing work culture expect them to adapt. The organisations are becoming more focused, driven, and profit-oriented and seem pretty soul-less. Life within such organisations is forever clouded by the possibilities of takeovers, merger, or acquisition giving rise to uncertainty all over.

We have travelled a long distance from even half a generation ago (10-15 years) when an international call had to be booked in advance. As public relations officer in my university, I was provided with an official telephone at my residence – the only one in my block of ten houses – no more now, when every house has a telephone, some of them mobile phones. STDs have become quite common. Air travel and going abroad for education, work or leisure is becoming frequent.

Teenagers are becoming so adept at the use of mobile phones that even middle-aged people feel inhibited and left-out from the ever evolving social and cultural milieu.

Portability of electronic communication technologies has led to the growth of tele-working. *A mobile phone, and electronic organiser and a seat at a café table, constitute a new work place. Work starts when the phone is switched on (The 24-Hour Society).* As Internet connections grow, our notions of what is local, national or international will get blurred.

The result of all these changes has been that the individual feels anxious and pressurised. We have started hearing more and more of BOSS (Burn-Out Stress Syndrome) in the context of work-related problems of call-centre employees. The employees of call centres – another gift of globalisation – have to pick up phones within a certain number of rings. Many youngsters can't handle the stress and errors pile up against their names. They start suffering from sleeping disorders, eye-fatigue, anxiety, lethargy, depression and several other work-related disorders including feeling of alienation.

The nature of work in a journalism career has changed quite fast over a period of past 10 years. Intense competition – to be first with breaking news – proliferation of news channels, online news and ubiquity of electronic technology has brought about new challenges. The pressure to design/ redesign a formula or the package to create something new, attractive and appealing for the readers and the audience increases every single day.

These are some of the manifestations of globalisation – a process which is speeding up and becoming more and more inexorable. In the final analysis, we will have to understand all its nuances and come up to face the challenges and opportunities it offers.

REFERENCES

Giddens, Anthony (2000), *Runaway World – How Globalisation is reshaping our lives*, Profile books, London.

Kingsnorth Paul (2003), *One No, Many Yeses – A Journey to the heart of the Global resistance movement*, Simon and Schuster UK Ltd., London.

Leon Kreitzman(1999), *The 24-Hour Society*, Profile Books, London.

4

NEW INFORMATION AND COMMUNICATION TECHNOLOGIES

Multimedia, Satellite Communication, Internet and its Social Impact

Since early 1960's Information Revolution has been the buzz word. The world has been experiencing, at an accelerating pace, an unprecedented Third Wave—fast forward movement. The Information Revolution is characterised by information becoming the central and most significant commodity. An interesting offshoot of the Information Revolution is—Informatization of Society on the one hand and the Commodification of Information on the other.

The significance of dawn of Information Revolution is underlined by the number of information-related terms it has given rise to : 'Information Society, Information Technology, Informatics, Information Industries, Informatization, Informatization Indicators and several more. Information has become a catalyst for economic development, and a key resource for literacy, education and social development. During the past five years or more there has been a flood of writings about information explosion.' 'Multi-media revolution' and 'information super highway', in relation to developments in Information Technology.

INFORMATION SOCIETY

The concept of Information Society goes back to the Japanese who are generally given credit for coining the Japanese term *Johoka Shakai* in mid-1960s. The term simply means Information Society, in which the primary activity of a majority of workforce is in the areas of information production, processing and distribution. In the Information Society, information constitutes the basic resource and information workers are the main segment of employees. Whereas the social scientists consider Information Society as a process of technical change, subsequently it has been defined in terms of workforce structure. In the Information Society, a majority of workforce is engaged in the production, processing, transmission and distribution of information goods and services. The bewildering advances and developments in computerised information systems have brought the industrialised nations to the brink of what some have begun to describe as post-industrial era of the Information Society. The centrality of information/knowledge has also been emphasised by Daniel Bell.

In the post-industrial society, processing of information will be more important than production of goods. The value of information will be increasingly recognised, as well as the need for information specialists to act as guides to the vast information resources that will exist in the electronic form. The magnitude and diversity of the electronic resources will place trained information workers in great demand. The ascendancy of information as commodity is becoming apparent even in developing countries, in that majority of labour force in quite a few of these countries consists of information workers. Informatization is becoming a global trend. Information is considered not only as a commodity but also as a cultural and social resource. The contemporary society is at a point where information and wealth are practically one and the same thing; information is a commodity rather than a public service.

An Information Society is a society characterized by abundant information in terms of both stock and flow, quick and efficient distribution and transformation of information, and easy and inexpensive access to information for all members of society. The Ministry of Posts & Telecommunications in Japan (1985) also indicated some of the key features of information as follow:

(a) Public needs for information have become increasingly sophisticated and diversified,

(b) New communication media share certain border areas with conventional media such as mail, telecommunications and broadcasting, and
(c) Networks (i.e. data communications) are being formed on a large scale.

The National Information Technology Plan for Singapore defines Information Technology as the use of computers, telecommunications and office systems in all aspects of information flow from collection and processing to storage, package and dissemination. Information technology, therefore, constitutes an integral component of the economic development plan of Singapore. It plays a dual role in the economic development of Singapore. It is a high tech industry in itself creating IT related products and services, as also a tool to increase productivity and enhance competitiveness in all sectors of society.

Alvin Toffler and Third Wave Media

The Information Age *guru* Alvin Toffler considers contemporary societal changes and technological developments as high speed revolution, the Third Wave, which is creating a new civilization all around us. Classifying agricultural phase as the First Wave, industrial phase as the Second Wave, he considers exploding change—with personal lives being torn apart, the existing social order crumbling, and a fantastic new way of life emerging on the horizon, as the Third Wave, with new life styles, new values and technologies, new modes of communication, new ideas and concepts emerging all around.

The Third Wave media analysis of Toffler underlines the diversity and intensity of Information Society wherein entertainment, information and leisure are dominated by the products of Information Technology.

New Information and Communication Technologies (NICT)

It is fascinating to observe that whereas the developing countries are still coming to terms with socio-economic and cultural implications of proliferation of mass media broadly classified as print and electronic media; the rapid advances made in Information Technology products, (the hardware which is the backbone of information society), New Media emerged in the late 1970. In the paper, *Information Society in their Mind* – A survey of college students in seven nations [*Asian Journal of Communication*, I, (II), 1991] Georgette Wang lists the ten items as New Media : one way and interactive cable television, video cassette recorders, video disc players, videotext, teletext, fascimile, personal computers, direct broadcast satellite and cellular radio.

The study, essentially explorative in nature revealed that awareness and knowledge among college students of different countries about New Media and Information Society varied greatly and reflected the extent and the degree to which the economies of their countries were industrialised.

Ten years after the opinion survey was completed, the situation had substantially changed. The New Media, particularly in India – facsimile, personal computers, cellular telephones – have expanded fast. Their application in various fields – teaching and training, literacy, distance education, financial institutions and other spheres has become increasingly conspicuous.

The New Media, are now generally classified as New Information and Communication Technologies (NICT). In his paper, New Information/Communication Technologies : Their Role in Education [*Media Asia,* 22 (2)], Kiran Karnik lists photocopying, video recording, facsimile, personal computers, E-mail and computer networks, satellite, telecommunication, including mobile communication and satellite broadcasting and receiving equipment for satellite transmissions as NICTs.

Some of these, like photocopying have been in use for many years, what is new is their present form, speed, accessibility and user-friendliness. However, with the phenomenal advances in communication technologies, the concept of 'new' is becoming controversial. This is particularly so because changes are so spectacular that what is new today may become archaic tomorrow, owing to the rapid changes in the industry. It is also apparent that more and more writers on communication technology are using the term 'Information and Communication Technology' or 'New Information/ Communication Technologies', interchangeably, rather than separate the technologies of information and communication. The convergence of both the technologies is such that it is difficult to distinguish the respective product application of one from the other. Each of them serves various functions but they share some common features. They disseminate messages with greater speed, accuracy and efficiency.

NICTs and Learning Society

The closing decade of the 20th century has witnessed the exponential growth in the ambit and application of communication technologies which have far-reaching relevance to education, its expansion and quality. The implications of the growth in communication technologies impacting the very nature of learning process and education system, are equally far-reaching, necessitating a continuous reassessment with respect to its effectiveness and scope. The traditional roles assigned to school, classroom and teacher and the expectation of the society in terms of quality of education are changing at a very fast pace. Concepts like the Learning Society, Interactive Technologies, Collaborative Learning, Knowledge Industries and Virtual University are not only transforming the way education is being imparted but it also changing the transmission of education itself.

The NICTs have brought human kind face-to-face with fundamental changes : by abolishing distances they are instrumental in shaping the societies of tomorrow; the most accurate, up-to-date information (in fact information as the events are developing) is now available to anyone, anywhere in the world, often in real time and reaches the remotest regions.

The dramatic emergence of information societies has led to a revolution in communications in the shape of multimedia systems and the spectacular expansion of information technology networks, including Internet. Even though the impact of the expansion of Internet is still limited in developing countries, owing to the relatively small number of people with the necessary technology know-how; everything suggests that an unstoppable revolution is in progress which will make it possible to transmit an ever-increasing mass of information in shorter span of time. At the same time, thanks to the falling cost of equipment, the new technologies are steadily finding their way into every aspect of work.

As the world moves towards a knowledge-based, post-industrial information society, the crucial importance of education becomes self-evident.

In his book, *The Death of Distance,* Frances Cairncross points out : The death of the distance as a determinant of the cost of communicating will probably be the single most important force shaping society in the first-half of the next century. Technological change has the power to revolutionize the way people live, and this one will be no exception. It will alter, in ways that are only dimly imaginable, decisions about where people work and what kind of work they do, concepts of national borders and sovereignty, and patterns of international trade. The death of distance will also give rise to proliferation of ideas. New ideas and information will travel faster to the remotest corner of the world. The Third World countries will have access to knowledge that the industrial world has long enjoyed.

At a time when knowledge industries are taking off at top speed, education has to be seen as a factor of crucial importance even as a part of economic development.

MULTIMEDIA

Today, it looks as if the word multimedia is sweeping the globe. Technologists, planners and policy-makers seem fascinated to talk about the bright future ahead—the dream world of the 21st century with the utilization of multimedia. Multimedia refers to the linkage of computers, television sets and telephones in an increasingly elaborate global network.

The electronic world is referred to as information highway, because of its potential to tap a vast realm of digitized information : stock market information, magazines, shopping catalogues, libraries – much of which is available on the Internet. It is the boundless worldwide web of computer networks.

The consulting agency, Booz-Allen and Hamilton, in a report to the office for the assessment of technological consequences of the Bundestag, the German House of Representatives, has characterised multimedia as a generic term for a wide variety of new types of products in the computer, telecommunication and media fields.

The fundamental multimedia characteristics, according to this report are interactive usage, the integration of various media types and digital technology. Interactive usage means that the user is not only a recipient but by using the relevant channels can recieve feedback and thereby change contents, respectively trigger actions. Integration of various media types means that video and audio sequences can be combined with text and data. Digital technology is used both for storage and later processing of the data on which the media are based.

The most commonly stated advantage of multimedia for Asia and the Pacific countries is that because it enables any remote region to receive information without delay, its utilization will be most useful in countries with vast land areas or mountainous and complex topography. Moreover, in the multimedia society receivers can also act as senders, whereas traditional media, such as TV, radio or books can only carry information one way, from senders to its receivers. Such an unprecedented Information Revolution will change the flow of people, their awareness and even social structures.

It should, however, be noted that it takes a tremendous amount of money to build the infrastructure necessary for the application of multimedia and equally huge amounts of energy to maintain the systems.

INFORMATION TECHNOLOGY

Today's advanced information communication technologies are not only the key carriers and processors of information content, but are increasingly vital technologies for economic development. They provide an indispensable infrastructure for all industrial production processes. They are also 'synergetic' i.e. they lead to growth in many other industries. They create an elaborate infrastructure around their products and services, similar to the automobile industry earlier in this century.

The former US Vice-President Gore advocated the "National Super Highway", to be realised by the year 2015. Likewise in Japan there is a plan to spread the same type of network system as in US by 2010. Similar plans have also been announced in Europe, China and Russia.

It would be interesting to recall the glowing euphoria, that accompanied the launching of the Early Bird Satellite by the US scientists in May 1965—heralded by the *Time* newsmagazine in its cover page story (May 14, 1965)—The Communications Explosion. Visualising a startling communication explosion ahead, the science feature on Electronics succinctly predicted a series of developments in medicine, world-wide telephoning, data fascimile transmission, educational TV and several kinds of entertainment offering choice of programmes and more. At the same time the glowing euphoria was tempered with caution. It was pointed out; whether or not the spread of such scientific largesse will indeed "save the world" is a problem that would not be solved by scientists alone. The sociological implications are immense. The analysis added : "I doubt if more food will be grown in India," says RAND Corp. Sociologist Joseph Goldsen, "even if every village gets a television set with lecturers teaching new agricultural techniques every hour. It takes generations to change customs and traditions."

This precisely is the dilemma that modern day communication scholars, sociologists, planners and policy-makers have to face—whether, and the extent to which information and communication technologies could serve the Third World countries in confronting their social and economic problems. If any, the scepticism and dilemma is being articulated with increasing concern.

Cultural Synchronization

The fear of cultural synchronization, in the wake of globalization of trade in cultural products and inceasing domination of USA in the production, distribution and consumption of cultural and media goods has been frequently articulated. Cultural synchronization essentially implies that the traffic of cultural products goes massively in one direction, consequently local inventiveness and creativity of the recepient culture is thrown into confusion or destroyed. This fear has been further accentuated when we take note of the surge in the overall American trade position of audio-visual products. After all the cultural industries, which include movies, TV serials are 'second' only to the aerospace industry in terms of their contribution to the American exports. To quote *Media Development* (1994, p. 4) :

> The scramble for the media and information market is reminiscent of the scramble for territory in colonial times. Except that this war is being won and lost in corporate boardrooms, on the stock market, in the financial corridors of the world and finally in the hyper-saturated media environments of our lives.

The information technology products have greatly contributed to this fear amongst Third World countries, which frequently finds expressions in the writings of media scholars and policy planners.

TECHNOLOGICAL LEAPFROGGING—SATELLITE TECHNOLOGY

Ever since the launching of the Early Bird Satellite in 1965 the satellite technology has been the prime mover in accelerating developments in the area of communication technologies. The Third World countries find satellite technology particularly relevant to their development needs as it helps them leapfrog obsolescent technologies.

Arthur C. Clarke, the eminent author of the science fiction book *Movie 2001 : A Space Odyssey*, distinguished scholar and science writer was the first to visualise the potential of satellites for the developing countries. Developing countries stand to gain most from these innovations as they are not yet burdened with heavy fixed investments in technology that is rapidly becoming obsolete. In one of the articles – New Communication Technologies and the Developing World, Clarke wrote :

> But why do we need such huge satellites, what have they got to do with the problems of the Third World? The answer may seem paradoxical, even perverse. In highly developed regions like the United States and much of Europe, communication satellites are a great convenience but are not absolutely vital. These countries already have excellent cable and microwave links.
>
> To many developing countries, however, satellites are essential, they will make it unnecessary to build the elaborate and expansive ground systems required in the past. Indeed, to such countries, satellites could be a matter of life and death. To put it as dramatically as possible, unless major investments are made in space, millions are going to die, or eke out brief and miserable lives. And most of those millions will be in the Third World.

The eminent Indian space scientist and visionary Vikram Sarabhai, who was primarily responsible for leading India into a modern technological direction said : A developing nation following a step by step approach towards progress is landed with units of small size, which do not permit the economic development of new technologies. Through undertaking ventures of uneconomic size with obsolete technologies, the race with advanced nations is lost before it is started. Developing nations such as India have the possibility of effectively using space communications for national needs. Compared to advanced nations they have indeed an advantage though not having an existing major investment in older technologies.

Global communications systems have been transformed radically during the 20-30 years due to a whole clusters of significant innovations in information technology. Probably the most important catalyst in this respect was the development of satellite technology. The use of satellites for commercial telecommunications dates only from 1965, when the Early Bird or Intelsat I satellite was launched. It was the first 'geostationary' satellite, located above the Atlantic Ocean and capable of carrying 240 telephone conversations or two television channels simultaneously. Since then the carrying capacity of the communications satellites has grown exponentially. Intelsat IV carried 6,000 simultaneous telephone conversations; Intelsat V carries 12,000 as well as television channels; Intelsat VIII (launched in 1995) carries 22,500 two-way telephone circuits and three television channels. The Intelsat system is a multi-nation consortium of 122 countries whose satellites are positioned to provide complete global coverage. In addition to Intelsat, there are regional systems, such as Eutelsat, which serves Europe, and others in Asia, Latin America and the Middle East and also private satellite systems, such as the PanAm Global Satellite System. The PanAm system was the first private system to provide global satellite services.

Satellite technology, together with a whole host of other communications technologies, is making possible quite remarkable levels of global communication of conventional messages and also the transmission of data. In this respect, the key element is the linking together of computer technologies with information-transmission technologies over vast distances. It has become possible for a message to be transmitted in one location and received in another on the other side of the world virtually simultaneously.

CABLE TELEVISION

Much like the satellite technology, development of cable television was also heralded as 'an answer to the need for more diversified content', since cable television offers the possibility of unlimited number of channels for a multiplicity of users and purposes (multiple channels, multiple choices for the viewer) it was trumpeted as 'technology of abundance'. It was, however, not adequately realised that cable television could not be optimally used unless there are a number of stations with a variety of programme material available to feed those channels. In the absence of sufficient quantity of culturally compatible, civic and community oriented software available, the cable operators have to fall back upon whatever is available in the entertainment supermarket.

One of the most favoured aspects of cable television is the availability of channels for educational and community access programming. In some countries where cable has been introduced, the regulatory authorities have made it a prerequisite that cable system operators, whether public or private provide a community or public access channel which citizens of the community can use for local interest programming.

THE INFORMATION SOCIETY – A RETROSPECTIVE VIEW

In their seminal book, the *Information Society – A Retrospective View* (1993), Herbert S. Dordick and Georgette Wang have made an attempt to revisit the claims that have been made for the emerging information society. One of the paragraphs reproduced below heralds the dawn of a new millennium, a brave young world, full of promise and prosperity.

The explosive diffusion of computers, telecommunication, broadcast and video media, and the information media is seen in national and global statistics. Almost half of the workers in the industrialized world are employed by the rapidly growing information industries, and in almost every industry there are workers, whose primary tasks are to create, collect, process, and distribute information. The value added information products and services to the United States GNP is today slightly greater than 45 per cent and for Europe and Japan somewhat more than 40 per cent. The world information industry, even if narrowly defined, will be greater than $ 500 billion before the end of the decade. The production, processing, and distribution of information is a major industry throughout the world.

However, doubts and scepticism sets in almost immediately as to the efficacy of the newly emerging dispensation to the Third World nations. The nagging issues of widening gulf between the information-rich and the information-poor as also between the haves and have-nots start emerging as under :

If there is a growing gap between the production and consumption of information there is, perhaps, an even greater gap between what have come to be known as the information-rich and the information-poor. Information technology and modern telecommunications raised renewed hopes for enhancing national development.

However, the gap between the developed and lesser developed nations continues to widen annually. Can these Third World nations ever catch up?

The planners and policy-makers throughout the Third World are faced with a dilemma, as to the extent to whcih new information and communication technologies can be usefully harnessed to solve the problems of underdevelopment. To resolve this dilemma, bold decisions and options will have to be taken, the choice to be made are economic and technological but also political in the first instance. Political decisions must be made in order to avoid some of the unforeseen economic and technological implications.

Two members of the International Commission for the Study of Communication Problems, Gabriel Garcia Marquez and Juan Somavia in their general comments to the Report said: There is a tendency in different parts of the Report to "glorify" technological solutions to contemporary communication problems. We want to emphasize that the "technological promise" is neither neutral nor value free. Decisions in this field have enormous political and social implications. Each society has to develop the necessary instruments to make an evaluation of alternative choice and their impact. The insistence on the need to develop communication infrastructures in Third World countries is correct and necessary, but it should not be overstated. It is not possible to solve contemporary communication problems through money and training alone.

ADVENT OF INTERNET

There are few other innovations, with as far-reaching consequences and comparable importance which have impacted the life and living styles as Internet in the contemporary society.

The advent of Internet has been so pervasive and all embracing at least in the developed world that it has given rise to new ideology – 'Internetphilia'. Although to some discerning critics, this ideology seems to be over-hyped, accompanied by irrational exuberance, others see in the Internet the cure for a number of ills besetting the contemporary society.

The descriptions about the use and utility of Internet seem to be written in hyperbolic language.

> Organisations are finding that the Internet is not just a new way to communicate. It is a market place where they can put orders out for bids, it is an instant newspaper for its staff, it is an ever order facility for its customers plus an endlessly updates inventory of those customers' likes and dislikes. In theory, it reduces the cost of every business process that involves information, be it a plan, and advertisement, a set of accounts, a request for supplies or a schedule of deliveries. Organisations do not have to own everything any more; they can be virtually integrated instead, connecting the different bits and pieces through this new medium. B2B, or Business to Business is a real future of Internet and it will transform our organisations.
>
> (Charles Handy in the *Elephant and the Flea: Looking Backwards to the Future)*.

Internet has suddenly accelerated the pace of change. Charles Handy, in the above book says: David Grayson of Britain's Business in the Community has come up with a neat summary of the pace of change. All of the world's trade in 1949 happens in a single day today, all the foreign exchange dealings in 1979 happen now in a single day, as do all the telephone calls made around the world in 1984, a year in a day is exactly how it feels sometimes.

INTERNETPHILIA

In an excellent contribution—the political economy of the Internet, Korinna Patelis shows that socio-economico-political factors determine online communication and largely control the future of Internet. The ideology of Internet - Internetphilia has been announcing the inevitable arrival of a whole new era, whose features are dramatically different, whose qualities and mechanisms cannot be understood with past methods of analysis. It clearly perpetuates a notion of clear break with the past. It is a qualitative change the motor engine of which is purely technological. The change, in turn, installs a new mode of producing, distributing and consuming information - transition from analog to digital information. The key to new era is the ability to store information in combinations of 1 and 0. The basic qualities possessed by the Digital Technology are *newness* and *dynamism*. Everything is new, everything is in constant fast movement.

Some other characteristics claimed for Internet are: Its global nature (because it annuls distances and removes the limitations of geography), the capacity to empower individuals, institutions and countries of socio-economic periphery and also to transform citizens across the globe from orthodox media couch-potatoes to active producers of online information. Such empowerment is enabled by the fact that Internet is decentralised: it has no centre and thus, it cannot be controlled.

It is argued that Internet gives rise to a whole new financial environment, a new economy. It is a digital economy based on abundance rather than scarcity, a market where supply equals demand and prices are set at the lowest optimum level; where oligopolies are avoided owing to low market entry costs; where market dysfunctions are history and diversity is guaranteed. This market is a producer and consumer paradise. Its hallmark is dynamic competition.

In Bill Gates words: Capitalism, demonstrably the greatest of the constructed economic systems, has in the past decade clearly proved its advantages over the alternative systems. As the Internet evolves into its broadband, global interactive network, those advantages will be magnified. Products and service providers will see what buyers want a lot more efficiently than ever before and consumers will buy more efficiently.

The article then goes on to enlist the Internet inequalities and points out that to a large extent telecom capacity and infrastructure will determine Internet usage growth. A country's existing telecommunication infrastructure is paramount for the growth of Internet usage; both providing capacity to ISPs and in providing users with domestic lines for dial-up usage. In addition, connection bandwidth is important for the speed of transmission, which varies significantly across the globe. It is well known that dedicated connections of high speed that accommodate large information flows are not available to the average user. Bandwidth variations mean that not all users have the same distribution system at their disposal: since without bandwidth there is no distribution of content*.

Internet—A Cause for Concern

The use of Net for questionable purposes has given rise to continuing concern throughout the world. Here are a number of instances in all situations: Laying claim to insider knowledge of companies, identification of 'hate sites' and its use as playground for paedophiles:

- In February 2000, a small British coffee roasting company called the Coburg group, valued at £2.5 million saw its share price multiply seven times on the rumours that it was about to launch an Internet venture. When the board denied the rumour the price dropped back. But by that time the pumpers had taken their profits and dumped their shares. Such instances of unfair trading and profit-making in the new economy shares during the eBusiness boom period in late nineties in India contributed to the collapse of share market in the country.

* This section of Internet draws on the article, *The Political Economy of the Internet* by Korinna Patelis in *Media Organisations in Society*, edited by James Curran.

- In 1996, the US Congress passed the Communications Decency Act, which made it a Federal Crime to put obscene and indecent words or images on the Internet. The concern was to protect children from pornography. However, next year the US Supreme Court invalidated a key provision of the law and ruled that in seeking to protect children, the law violated the rights of adults.
- In 1997 itself, the Wiesenthal Centre identified more than 500 **'hate sites'**. Their 1999 report identified 1426 sites including an online video game whose objective was to lynch a black man. The first federal prosecution of an Internet hate crime materialised in 1996, when a 19-year old former student at the University of California sent an email message to about 60 Asian students. Signed as 'Asian Hater', the email ordered the students to leave the campus or be killed by him. He was convicted in 1998 of interfering with students' civil rights to attend a public university.
- A classics teacher at the famous Eton College, was arrested in February 2004 for hoarding a library of 2000 child porn pictures on his school computer. He had to resign from the top school, where princes William and Harry had been former students. When asked why he had assembled the collection, the accused said that he had saved the images because they were attractive to him and he wanted to look at them again. The teacher was sentenced to 9-months in prison to be suspended for two years for his voyeuristic behaviour.
- A former Crown Court judge in UK, who had also worked in the Army attaining the rank of Major General was sentenced to 12-months community rehabilitation order for storing 75 pornographic images of the boys on his laptop computer. The former judge, who is married with four children and six grandchildren said that he had visited the child porn sites out of curiosity. The police said, "I hope this case sends a clear message to the general public that the police will pursue and bring before the courts anyone who downloads images of child abuse, whatever their explanation" (*The Guardian*, 14 July 2004)

- *Operation Ore 2002:* Of all the cases, the most disturbing ones related to investigations into the users of online child pornography in Britain. Tracking the credit card customers of an illegal sites in Texas, the UK police arrested more than 3500 people, 1700 people charged and 1200 people convicted, with 1300 investigations still going on. The two detailed articles, one of them by a senior journalist who rose to become the online editor of *The Times* wrote that 'Pornography was endemic on the Internet and one developed an appetite for this. In the shocking account, the author of the article in the *Times Magazine* (17 July 2004), Andy Bull explains how his obsessive use of online pornography spiralled out of control and into images of pictures of teenage girls. When he entered indirect terms such as Lolita into search engines, tens of thousands of sites of likely illegality were presented for him. Bull asks, 'If I committed a crime in making those search requests, why did the owners of the search engines not commit a crime in providing search results to me'. To the readers it seems to be a perfectly normal affair when he says, 'I was able to go online with British Telecom, find child pornography through Google and pay for it with Visa Card'.

Children and Use of Internet

Children are growing up with the Internet as a normal part of life, using it at home, with friends and at school and exploring its amazing possibilities. The Internet has become a vital tool for communication, information, entertainment and shopping and is critical for children's development in today's world. Most schools in UK are now connected to the Internet and when the child goes on to further education or a job he will almost certainly be expected to be a confident user of computers and the Internet.

Children visit web sites, including chat rooms through mobile phones, the portable PC—the Internet at their fingertips wherever they are. The newest mobile phones let them take photos, make mini film clips and send them via email.

The *Home Office,* UK, in its information brochure, has provided guidelines to the parents to keep children safe on Internet. Parents must ensure that children are careful before they send images of themselves or friends to others using a mobile phone. Digital images can be easily manipulated, put onto a website and sent to millions of people at the click of a button.

Children use the Internet to :

- *Find Out Information :* The Internet is an incredible source of information on almost any topic. Search engines allow an individual to type in a few keywords, names or dates and receive hundreds of links to the subject we are interested in. Children are often encouraged at school to research topics on the Internet, and will often turn first to educational or other websites to get information for coursework or homework.
- *Get in Touch with Others :* Emails, Instant Messaging (IM) and chat rooms are probably the best known ways for making online friends and staying in touch with people over the Internet. But it is also possible to swap files, films or music, enter discussion groups and play interactive games online. Making contact over the Internet is very popular among children, who see it as a fun and adventurous extension to their social lives.
- *Play Online Games :* Gaming means playing interactive games. It is one of the most popular reasons for children using the Internet. They can either download a game from a website to play or visit a website to play with others who are online - either friends or strangers who are connected to the Internet at the same time. To do this, children need either an Internet-enabled games console or a computer connected to the Internet, and there is usually a monthly subscription fee.
- *Buy Online :* The Internet links an individual to thousands of companies, organisations and individuals with something to sell. Some of these are well-known

high-street companies, which have online sites, but it is also possible to buy items from individuals all over the world through online auctions. Children can buy books, games, CDs, videos, toys or collectibles online, although one usually needs a credit card to do this.

Risks of Internet

Because children cannot see the person they contact on-line, they have no idea if they are who they say they are. Chat rooms are particularly popular with children and teenagers, and there is a risk that paedophiles or sex abusers might use them to look for victims. They might pose as children or teenagers, try to strike up a friendship and eventually try to persuade them to meet up. Even if an adult is honest about his age, that is no guarantee of his good intentions.

Surfing the Internet from the comfort or safety of home or through a mobile phone can give a false sense of security. Children can unwittingly give away personal details such as where they live or go to school, or even begin to trust someone they don't know and willingly give them personal contact details. In contacting people over the Internet, children may also inadvertently give out their email address, which increases the risk of receiving unwanted emails. These emails, known as spam, may contain unsuitable material or even viruses that can damage the computer.

The vast majority of material on the Internet is legal, decent and honest. But it is easy to find, or even to stumble across, information or images that may be unsuitable for children. This could include pornography, or material that is violent, racist, inaccurate, or harmful in some other way. There is also Internet material that is clearly illegal, such as images of child abuse.

SEARCH ENGINES

Search engines are the market makers of the Internet. They connect consumers with providers at the very moment of consumer interest and enable all of us to find exactly what we want, when we want it. They bring great efficiency to the Internet and our lives and shall exist as long as the network of servers and computers we call the Web is around.

The first purpose of search engine optimization is to be positioned in the places where your customer is. The second purpose is to be positioned better than your competitors in these places. In the world of search engines, better means higher, and higher means a much greater probability that an individual will click on your link.

Ninety per cent of people looking for websites come through a handful of search engines. The important ones are: Google, Yahoo, MSN, AOL, AskJeeves, Overture, Infospace, Netscape and AltaVista. There are hundreds of other search engines, but these are the ones that require special effort to attain those top rankings for your keyword phrases. Some of the important search engines are:

Google(http://www.google.com) Voted three times 'Most Outstanding Search Engine' by Search Engine Watch readers, Google has a well deserved reputation as the top choice for those searching the web. The crawler-based service provides both comprehensive coverage along with great relevance. It is highly recommended as a first stop in your hunt for whatever you are looking for.

Google provides the option to find more than web pages, however. Using the "tabs" on the top of the search box on the Google home page, one can easily seek out images from across the web, discussions that are taking place on Usenet newsgroups, and scan through human compiled information provided from the Open Directory

Google was originally a Stanford University project by students Larry Page and Sergey Brin called BackRub. By 1998, the name had been changed to Google, and the project jumped off campus and became the private company Google.

MSN Search (http://search.msn.com) MSN Search is a shining example of the company putting that same effort into an online product. The company has its own team of editors that monitors the most popular searches being performed and then hand-picks sites that are believed to be the most relevant. After performing a search, "Popular Topics" shown below the search box on the results page are also suggestions built largely by editors to guide you into making a more refined search. When appropriate, search results may also feature links to encyclopaedia content from Microsoft Encarta or news headlines, at the top of the page.

MSN Search provides a blend of directory information and crawler coverage different from any of the other top choices. It is a high quality resource that provides its own unique view of the web and one worth checking.

Management Information System

Information systems designed for structured flow of information and integrating EDP jobs by business functions and generating reports from a database.

Systems that provide timely, reliable, and useful information to managers in business, industry, and government. MIS specialists apply the theoretical concepts of computer science to real-world, practical business problems.

Content Management Systems

Software that enables one to add and/or manipulate content on a Website. Typically, a CMS consists of two elements: the content management application (CMA) and the content delivery application (CDA). The CMA element allows the content manager or author, who may not know HTML, to manage the creation, modification, and removal of content from a Web site without needing the expertise of a Webmaster. The CDA element uses and compiles that information to update the Website. The features of a CMS system vary, but most include Web-based publishing, format management, revision control, and indexing, search, and retrieval.

A content management system is a system used to manage the content of a website. It typically consists of two elements: the content management application (CMA) and the content delivery application (CDA). The CMA allows the author, to manage the creation, modification, and removal of content from a website. The CDA element compiles the information to update the website. The features of a CMS vary, but most include format management, search, web-based publishing, revision control, and indexing, and retrieval.

Convergence

Convergence refers to two different trends :

Convergence between the broadcasting and tele-communications sectors

Advances in technology make it possible to use different media (cable networks, terrestrial and satellite radio relay systems, computer terminals and television sets) to carry and process all kinds of information and services, including sound, images and data. This type of convergence is due to a revolution in technology (digitisation). It has economic and regulatory implications.

Fixed/mobile convergence

Increasingly similar technologies are used and services provided by fixed telephone and mobile telephone systems. This type of convergence opens up prospects for operators to propose the same services to all users, regardless of the technology or networks they use.

There is no doubt that NICTs, satellite communication and Internet have brought about revolutionary changes in our personal lives, the society and the media industry. However there seems to be a great deal of hype associated with it.

Some media commentators have gone to the extent of saying that, "The gutenberg era is over. A new digital communications technology has emerged. An electronic superhighway is beginning to girdle the globe as voice, video and data converge, bringing in their wake a new basket of digital, multimedia and interactive communication technologies."

It appears that media have suddenly opened up. An instance has been cited wherein a company in USA which had been facing a barrage of insinuations about one of its edible products, answered them :–

1. On its own website
2. On a telephone helpline
3. A helpdesk-to answer questions raised in print media.
4. Through third party websites.

It would, therefore, be essential for the practitioners and users of media to be aware of the possibilities that the new media offer in the global media environment.

REFERENCES

Clarke, Arthur C. (1981), New Communication Technologies and the Developing World. *Media Asia* 185-190. (as reproduced in *Opening Windows-Issues in Communication,* The Silver Jubilee Collection, AMIC Singapore).

Dicken Peter (1998), *Global Shift: Transforming The World Economy,* Paul Chapman Publishing Ltd, London.

Dordick, Herbert S. and Wang. Georgette (1993), *The Information Society – A Retrospective View.* Sage Publications, New Delhi.

Frances Cairncross (1977), *The Death of Distance,* Harvard Business School Press, Boston.

Mowlana, Hamid and Wilson, Laurie J. (1988). Communication Technology and Development. UNESCO 101.

Time (1965), The Communications Explosion : Early Bird and After : Electronic – The Room Size World, pp. 48-51, 14 May.

Toffler, Alvin (1981), *The Third Wave.* Pan Books Limited, Cavaye Place, London.

NEW GLOBAL MEDIA

International Media Institutions, News Agencies and Alternate Media Organisations

The modern times have seen a proliferation and strengthening of international media institutions, news agencies, and alternate media organisations. Some of these like the BBC, the Reuters, AFP and CNN have been well established media institutions and news agencies working in the area of news production, dissemination and distribution for several decades, whereas alternate media organisations have come up during the recent years. All these institutions have contributed greatly in terms of disseminating news worldwide with different perspectives. Whereas it may be difficult to include all such international media institutions, the ones with wider reach and impact are discussed in this chapter.

BBC: The BEEB takes on the World

- The BBC programmes have been setting trends and breaking news for decades.
- For all its criticism, the BEEB is still widely admired, respected and listened to by more people around the world than ever. The corporation produces forty hours of output for each hour of the day on its domestic radio and TV networks, and 93 percent of Brits tune in at least once a week.
- The people coming down hardest on the corporation are its commercial competitors – particularly the global media baron, Rupert Murdoch. During the Hutton Enquiry into the suicide of weapon expert David Kelly – whose leak to Gillian prompted his explosive charge on the *'Today'*

programme that, ' The Downing Street put material in its Iraq weapon's Dossier probably knowing it was wrong' – Murdoch's papers turned their guns on BBC.

The above excerpts, from the cover page story of *'Time'* in its issue of 13 October 2003, by and large, sum up the pre-eminence that BBC – a first rate international radio and television media institution, enjoys worldwide.

The earliest provider of television journalism in the UK, the British Broadcasting Corporation began life in 1922 as the broadcasting company. Originally a cartel of radio manufacturers depending on licence fee and a share of royalties on the sale of radio receivers, the company was nationalised and became the British Broadcast Company in 1926.

In all countries in the world, the broadcasting activity was left to the newly organised broadcasting institutions which grew rapidly in 1920s.

BBC was shaped by John Reith who ensured that the structure of BBC was neither commercial nor government controlled. John Reith's name has been inextricably linked to Public Service Broadcasting. The first studios used by the BBC were at Alexandra Place, a North London Centre of 19th Century Entertainment.

It will be interesting to note the awe and esteem in which the BBC was held in its early years, described by Asa Briggs and Peter Burke in their book, A *Social History of the Media: From Gutenberg to Internet*, "The BBC was considered an institution rather than an organisation. A former editor of *Listener*, the BBC journal, R S Lambert in his book, *Ariel and all His Qualities*, had said, "In the field of art, intellect and politics, the BBC exercised through patronage all the power once exercised by the Court".

From the outset, Reith promoted the notion of public service and BBC as a cultural, moral, and educative force for the improvement of knowledge, taste and manners...'a powerful means for promoting social unity' and creating 'an informal and reasoned public opinion as an essential part of the political process in a mass democratic society. Broadcasting was to take on the task of establishing a common culture amongst the national audience.

In the meanwhile, spanning over a period of more than half a century, BBC has gone ahead from strength to strength in all its activities—online programming, educational broadcasting, world service, and programme production.

BBC Online

BBC online is one of the leading news sites, competing for global domination with CNN, Yahoo News, Fox.com, and others seeking to establish themselves as online providers of choice for the news hungry. According to the *Times* (6 July 2004): Its online educational material reaches 80% of UK schools and the corporation is launching a £150 million 'Digital curriculum', using video games to make learning compelling and exciting for school children.

Golden Reach of BBC

We also have another selling point: Our golden reach, the fact that we have correspondents in most of the places most of the time. Very few broadcasters can say that. When the Gulf War was on, we had 30 or 40 correspondents in the region, but we also covered events from Moscow, Africa, South America and so on. We produce a genuine world service. We have a global reach. We see the events of one country in terms of what is happening elsewhere...The world service aspires to genuinely global news agenda, of equal relevance to the constituent parts of a multi-national audience*.

The article in the *Time* magazine says: The BBC's international reach is the envy of broadcasters and governments throughout the rest of Europe. *BBC World,* the corporation's international News Channel, is now seen in 273 million households in more than 200 countries, up from 24 million homes when it was launched in 1995. BBC America is in 37 million American homes.

The above article quoted French President Jacques Chirac saying that - It was essential for the nation to have 24-hour international news channel on a par with BBC and CNN.

---

* McNair, in his book, *News and Journalism in UK*

Without one, the French voice is not sufficiently heard or understood in international affairs.

Public Value

The BBC charter is due for renewal in 2006. Because of this reason, and also as a result of criticism by the Hutton Commission, the BBC governors have come out with a manifesto in an attempt to work out a blueprint for its survival. In future, the BBC's value will be judged by public value – subdivided into democratic, cultural, educational, social and global values.

INTERNATIONAL NEWS AGENCIES

No newspaper, however well staffed it may be in terms of news-gathering, can hope to survive without the help of news agencies. News agencies bring in a constant flow of well-edited news messages from all over the world where the newspaper is not represented through its staff reporters or stringers. They never go to bed and are active and ticking every moment of the day and night.

News agencies in the USA are known as wire services. As we know the four major international news agencies/wire services that dominate the world are: APF (Agence France Presse); AP (Associated Press); UPI (United Press International) and the Reuter. Each of these wire services has offices in a large number of countries throughout the world. These agencies account for 80 per cent of the immediate international news. Their services are utilized by the newspapers, major TV networks and radio stations all over the world. The dependence of newspapers on wire services is underlined by the fact that news agencies bring them not only national and international news, but also cartoons, comic strips, crossword puzzles and news features.

AP's Prescription for Lead

The news agencies, right from the beginning, changed the very concept the way the news is being reported in the newspapers.

In this context the comments in *Understanding Mass Communication* are noteworthy: In the early days, sending stories by telegraph was very expensive and clarity and precision were essential. The correspondent in the field had less time for the flowery language and elongated sentences common to early nineteenth century newspapers. Before long, reporters and editors began to distinguish between 'telegraph' and 'newspaper' stories. The concise writing needed for wire stories eventually produced AP's famous prescription for a lead: "who, what, where, when and why." Stories transmitted by wire were organized in the inverted pyramid style, in which the most important elements were first, the next important second, and so on. Thus, if a local newspaper needed to save space, a story could easily be shortened by dropping less important details from the tail of the pyramid.

Since a news agency serves a variety of clientele—newspapers, electronic media networks, individuals and other media establishments—having varying ideologies and opinions on political, social and economic issues, it can hardly afford to deviate from the straight path of factual reporting. As a matter of policy, a news agency generally abstains from editorializing, commenting or interpreting, something so common in newspapers.

Reuters

Reuters takes its name from its founder, Julius Reuter, a Jew from Cassel Germany who set up the London organisation in October 1851, which eventually extended throughout the world.

During that period, London, in addition to being the financial centre of the Victorian World, it was also becoming the communication centre for a growing cable network. Free trade and a free press added to the atmosphere Reuter needed to succeed in its new venture*. By 1858, Reuter was offering general an political news received by telegraph from all over Europe, as well as financial information.

In 1889, they were to start a 'Special India and China service', and thereafter for almost a century India was destined

* London constituted the focal point of the rapidly developing international economy and 'Industrial Britain' was the *workshop of the world.*

to play a central part in the 'Reuter Empire within the British Empire', an Empire which came to depend on telegraphy.

Reuter is one of the largest of the international news agencies, with more than 70 bureaus around the world, supplying news by satellite to upwards of 200 broadcasters in 85 countries.

The American *Forbes* magazine (30 October 1989) observed: Not long ago Reuters was a poor but proud ward of the British newspaper industry, beset like the rest of the Fleet street by lousy labour relations and lazy management. No more. Reuters has turned itself into nothing less than the world's leading supplier of computerised information. The editor-in-chief from 1989, Mark Wood, made the point: Reuters is pacing the world.

While looking for material on Reuters, I came across an eminently readable book: *The Power of News: The History of Reuters*. On one of its inner pages, just before the preface, the following excerpts on full page makes an interesting reading:

> Vatican City, Sept. (1978), Reuter—Pope John Paul said today that if the early Christian Disciple St. Paul returned to the world he would head Reuters, the International News Agency.

A fitting tribute to the working and influence of the major news agency of the world.

During 1999, the Reuters had announced an agreement to combine their interactive business services for the corporate and professional markets in a joint venture called Factive. Next year it launched major initiatives to exploit the Internet and open new markets, reinforced by Joint Ventures in Communications, Wireless delivery and investment research.

Developed by Reuters and Microsoft, Reuters Messaging Service was launched in 2002. The service was specifically developed for the global financial services industry. The service allows financial professionals to communicate instantly with their colleagues and customers.

Reuters is the leading global provider of news, financial information and technology solutions to the world's financial institutions, businesses and the media. Its offerings include real time financial data; transaction capabilities, texts, graphics, video and pictures to media organisations world wide.

Agence France Presse (AFP)

Founded in 1835 by Charles-Louis Havas the father of global journalism, AFP is the world's oldest established news agency. According to the agency newsletter, AFP gained international fame for breaking news of Stalin's death in 1953.

The agency reaches thousands of subscribers—radios, TVs, newspapers, companies from its main headquarters in Paris and regional centers in Washington, HongKong, Nicosia and Montevideo. The stated goal of the agency is: to guarantee a top quality international service tailored for the specific needs of clients in each region.

In January 1957, the French Parliament adopted the AFP's status and it got new legal structure. In January 1985, it launched the international photoservice. Interestingly among the keydates the agency considers 27 September 1988 important when it scooped the world by two hours in announcing that Ben Johnson failed in a drug test resulting in his disqualification from the Seoul Olympic Games. In February 2000 the agency launched Olympic Games Multimedia Service.

Around the world it has journalists in 165 countries and the AFP team has more than 2000 staff, with 900 working outside France. The AFP products include 400,000-600,000 words in text, 700 photos and 50 news graphics.

Associated Press (AP)

The founding of the Associated Press dates from 1848, when ten men representing six New York newspapers met in the offices of *The New York Sun*. An agreement was reached to make efforts for collecting international news and to offset the prohibited cost of telegraph.

Among the important highlights mentioned by the agency include :

- 1858 cable containing 42 words summarizing five stories in headline: "Mutiny being quelled, all India becoming tranquil."
- AP agent Joseph L Gilbert takes down Abraham Lincoln's words at Gettysburg. The Gettysburg Address becomes

the most reliable account of the historical memorable three minutes.

- During the period 1945-50, several of AP correspondents were executed, arrested or captured.

  – War correspondent Joe Morton executed by Nazis at the Mauthausen concentration camp in 1945,
  – Its correspondent in Bacharest arrested by the Romanian communist authorities in 1950 and served 10 years of 25 years sentence for alleged spying.
  – Its photographer Frank Pappy Noel captured by North Korean soldiers in 1950 during the Korean War, freed in 1953.

- In 1967 it launched the AP-Dow Jones Economic Report for collecting financial news from around the world.
- In 1969, AP dispatched 70 editors, photographers, operators and technicians to Houston and Cape Kennedy to document Neil Armstrong's momentous step of landing on the moon.
- In 1994, it launched APTV, a global video news gathering agency and two years later it lauched. The Wire, a continuously updated news service on Internet combining text, photos, audio and video news.

United Press International (UPI)

The company was started by newspaper publisher E.W. Scripps in 1907 by combining three news services. The principle on which the news agency was founded was that there should be no restrictions on who could buy news from a news service.

The company is headquartered in Washington DC with offices in HongKong, London, Santiago, Seoul and Tokyo. It maintains a global network of correspondents to cover major stories round the world on topics which include finance, entertainment, sports, science as well as different geopolitical and sociological issues.

While going through its history, one is surprised at the number of its photographers and reporters who got pulitzer prizes for excellence in reporting ground breaking stories and taking photographs in Vietnam.

The first Pulitzer Prize was awarded to Russell Jones for the coverage of the 1956 Hungarian Revolution. In 1963, the UPI sent to the world the first bulletin on the assassination of President John Kennedy when its correspondent Merriman Smith grabbed the mobile radiophone in the motorcade's lead press car and dictated dispatches to UPI's Dallas bureau. He followed with a steady stream of reports from Parkland Hospital and later from Air Force One as Lyndon Johnson took oath of office and flew back to Washington. Smith's coverage, which won the 1964 Pulitzer Prize for National Reporting, has been called the finest example of deadline reporting in the 20th century.

In 2001, UPI developed a multi-lingual "virtual newsroom". Its middle east correspondents produce news and analysis stories in Arabic. The Latin American Bureau produces news of the region in Spanish language. Its products include UPI Perspectives, issue-focused news reports and in-depth reports, UPI News Track—a fast and snapshot of major stories, UPI Photos, UPI Spanish and UPI Arabic Service.

CABLE NEWS NETWORK (CNN)

The brain child of media and entertainment entrepreneur Ted Turner, CNN was launched from Atlanta, Georgia on 1 June 1980. Turner's idea of 24-hour cable news channel distributed by satellite across the US was the beginning of the "second age of television". According to an eminent media academic McNair, by utilising technological innovation, the nature of news and information broadcasting was fundamentally transformed. The uniqueness of the product ensured its survival.

The Gulf War—the first television war seen all over the world heralded the arrival of CNN as a world wide television news service. CNN was received in 100 countries across the globe and facilitated 24-hour coverage of war much of which was live television.

The eminent Indian journalist P. Sainath pointed out the attraction of CNN to the Indian elite and the domination of

Indian press and television by western pro-war sources. Most of the Gulf War news was a highly managed affair. The content analysis of CNN, Sky News and UK terrestrial television showed that over half of the coverage of War was studio-based.

Gulf War apart, TWA hijacking in 1985, US bombing of Libya were the other events through which CNN achieved an immediacy of coverage which no other organisation could match.

While putting Ted Turner as Man of the year in 1992, the *Time* magazine said, "CNN had changed the definition of news from being "some thing that has happened", to some thing that is "happening at the very moment you are hearing of it." The CNN news presentation stressed *immediacy.*

In 1995, Time Warner, which is one of the largest media corporations in the world acquired CNN.

ALTERNATIVE MEDIA

Aljazeera

Aljazeera was launched in November 1996. This channel has become a global name which people, governments, and decision-makers cannot afford to ignore.

Aljazeera gained world fame in the wake of 11 September terrorist attack in the US through its exclusive footage of video tapes of Osama Bin Laden and his al-Qaeda terror network.

Aljazeera emerged as an alternative source of information for the outside world which found coverage in the US and British press regarding war in Iraq too biased. It located journalists in the war zones and had greater access to the Iraqi towns and cities and, therefore, could report more independently than those journalists dependent on the armed forces for their personal safety and communication equipment. It depicted the war as 'War on Iraq' as against 'War in Iraq' adopted by the BBC, whereas Fox News adopted the Pentagon's depiction, 'Operation Iraqi Freedom'.

Writing for the publication: *Tell me Lies; Propaganda and Media Distortion in the attack on Iraq*, Faisal Bodi, Senior editor at Aljazeera.net and Columnist for *The Guardian*, specialising in

Muslim affairs says: From an early stage, the decision was made to fill the website with stories and features based on themes that reflected the concerns on the Arab streets rather than of western politicians. The humanitarian fallout of the invasion raised all kinds of issues : civilian casualties, toxic wastes from depleted uranium, refugees, ethnic and sectarian civil strife, and the further marginalisation of Palestinians.

It is, therefore, obvious that the coverage of conflict in Iraq differed qualitatively from those by the embedded journalists or who depended upon the briefings by the Qatar based US Central Command Media Complex.

Consequently the Baghdad Bureau of Aljazeera became the target of attack of US forces repeatedly. Its offices had been bombed by the US jets in Kabul, the Afghan capital two years earlier. Aljazeera has been paying a heavy price for its independent reporting, but during a short period of less than four years, it has emerged as a powerful source of information.

With more than 30 bureaus and dozens of correspondents covering the four corners of the world, Aljazeera has given millions of people a refreshing new perspective on global events.

Free from the shackles of censorship and government control Aljazeera has offered its audiences in the Arab world much needed freedom of thought, independence, and room for debate. Aljazeera's correspondents opened a window for the world on the millennium's first two wars in Afghanistan and Iraq. They continue to cover all viewpoints with objectivity, integrity and balance.

Aljazeera.net

Aljazeera.net is the online version of the Aljazeera. In January 2001, Aljazeera.net (Arabic) was launched as the first mainstream Arabic news site and in no time, it rose to the top of the Arab media. In 2002, Aljazeera.net (Arabic) received more than 811 million impressions and 161 million visits.

Indymedia

The Independent Media Centre (www.indymedia.org), was established by various independent and alternative media organizations and activists in 1999 for the purpose of providing grassroot coverage of the World Trade Organization (WTO) protests in Seattle. The centre acted as a clearinghouse of information for journalists, and provided up-to-the-minute reports, photos, audio and video footage through its website. Using the collected footage, the Seattle Independent Media Centre (seattle.indymedia.org) produced a series of five documentaries, uplinked every day to satellite and distributed throughout the United States to public access stations.

The centre also produced its own newspaper, distributed throughout Seattle and to other cities via the Internet, as well as hundreds of audio segments, transmitted through the web and Studio X, a 24-hour micro and Internet radio station based in Seattle. The site, which uses a democratic open-publishing system, logged more than 2 million hits, and was featured on America Online, Yahoo, CNN, BBC Online, and numerous other sites. Through a decentralized and autonomous network, hundreds of media activists setup independent media centres in London, Canada, Mexico City, Prague, Belgium, France, and Italy over the next year. IMCs have since been established on every continent, with more to come.

Indymedia is increasingly becoming a global network of locally controlled websites, radio stations and video projects and offers grass root and non-corporate coverage of events. Its favoured slogan is, *"Do not hate the media, become the media."*

It is a collective of independent media organizations with hundreds of journalists offering grassroot, non-corporate coverage. Indymedia is a democratic media outlet for the creation of radical, accurate, and passionate tellings of truth. The indymedia.org group manages an international Indymedia page and coordinates technical and editorial policy issues that affect all IMCs that are associated with the Indymedia network.

Indymedia is dedicated to providing a forum for independent reporting about important social and political issues. Several hundred media activists, many of whom have been working for years to develop an active independent media through their own organizations, came together in late November 1999 in Seattle to create an Independent Media Center to cover protests against the World Trade Organization. The Seattle IMC provided coverage of the WTO through both a printed publication called "The Blind Spot" and the first IMC website. In February 2000 a small IMC formed in Boston to cover the Biodiversity Conference and a larger one came together in Washington DC to cover protests against the World Bank and International Monetary Fund. After that requests from local groups interested in forming their own IMCs started to pour in. There are now over one hundred local Independent Media Centers around the world and more are on the way.

Indymedia endeavours to empower people to become the media by presenting honest, accurate, powerful independent reports. One vague long-term goal would be to foster and facilitate the development of as much independent media as possible around the world. Some come to Indymedia with a deeper goal, to enable people, while they're "becoming the media," to realize they can take control of other aspects of their lives. On a practical level, some who are involved with Indymedia are working towards the development of national and/or international television or radio networks, and others are working towards the establishment of an international independent regular newspaper and other projects that will assure the public has access to independent news reports.

Indymedia and the 'anti-globalization' movement: Free Trade versus Fair Trade

While Indymedia is not a conscious mouthpiece of any particular point of view, many Indymedia organizers and people who post to the Indymedia newswires are supporters of the "anti-globalization" (alternative globalization, anti-corporatization) movement. Corporate media often describe those who protest so-called "free trade" conferences and agreements as being "anti-globalization," ostensibly against the process of breaking down national borders to create what pro-globalization economists claim will be a more profitable world. This misrepresents the reality of the international movement for social justice, which advocates not the "free trade" of powerful governments (trade that allows goods and services to flow across national borders, often in a way that allows producers to move their manufacturing plants to countries where they can pay workers a pittance), but "fair trade" that opens borders to goods and people as a way of sharing the earth's natural and manufactured resources in a way that will benefit all. Today's social justice activists are not against globalization of community, justice and resources, they protest the economic globalization coordinated by the powerful few that results in their profiting from the work of the majority of the world's population. They sometimes prefer to call themselves "alternative globalization" activists, or those who are against the increasing corporatization of society and culture. Perhaps people who protest against the power of multinational corporations, faceless international financial institutions and inaccessible governments have over their lives found encouragement in Indymedia's newswire, which encourages them to present their own account of what is happening in the world. People participating in protests that question the very tenets of corporate domination of their lives understand why their issues are unlikely to receive honest consideration in the corporate-owned media. Activists planning an alternative globalization/anti-corporatization event can assure a safe space for presenting non-corporate news by forming a local IMC to provide coverage of the event, or posting news to the site of a local IMC that currently exists.

TRANSNATIONAL OLIGOPOLISTIC MEDIA MARKET

In the realm of international communication a new mass media environment has developed; since the 1990s this new order has brought about profound transformations. According to several media academics, whereas previously most of the media systems were primarily national, in the recent past a global commercial media market has emerged. This has been due to the formation of transnational multi-media conglomerates through various processes and strategies to enable them to consolidate their powerful positions on the global media map.

In a scholarly contribution to *The Oxford Companion to the Politics of the World,* media analyst Ben H. Bagdikian discusses how a single, large multinational media corporation can control the entire communication system from creation of content to distribution and delivery to home or office. This is done by ownership of newspapers, magazines, radio, television, books, motion pictures, video cassettes, production facilities for all these media, as well as national and international distribution networks and control of the telephone and satellite dish that brings media material into individual homes. Media power and profit have encouraged large firms to acquire as many different media as possible under each major firm's control.

The process of globalisation has also resulted in emergence of multinational media conglomerates operating across national boundaries. Some of these are :

News Corporation

Owned by the media tycoon, Rupert Murdoch, it has become a major media producer world wide and is the biggest English langauge newspaper publisher in the world. Its US TV stations reach 40 per cent of the viewing population. It has controlling interests in British Sky Broadcasting as well as America's fourth largest television network, Fox and STAR in Asia. STAR-TV has emerged as a very major force in Indian television system.

Bertelsmann

The Germany based firm controls ten per cent of all world publishing in English language, is the largest TV and radio firm in Europe and its BMG Music does considerable business in Asia. It owns Random House in the United States.

Disney

It has established a strong presence in Japan, China, Europe and Latin America. Its ESPN International is broadcast in 21 languages to 155 million households in 182 countries.

Time Warner

It is a major global player in virtually every media sector except newspapers and radio. Its two examples are CNN International which reaches 200 nations and HBO has expanded throughout Europe.

AT&T

Has holding in satellite, cable and broadcast television and owns stakes in Time Warner, News Corporation and CNBC.

Whereas it is difficult to analyse the implications of global media market on politics and economies of nations, it is becoming apparent that authoritarian governments find it difficult to control the corporate and private information sources from reaching out to the audiences. During the democracy movement in China in 1989, dissenting Chinese students maintained contact with the outside world through hundreds of fax machines. They succeeded in disseminating the news of military action against the students by the army in Tiananmen Square in Beijing.

Similarly collapse of the Soviet system and the Berlin Wall is credited to the proliferation of sources and channels of news.

International media institutions, news agencies and alternate media organisations all contribute to the pervasiveness of messages leading to an environment of information and entertainment overload. The presence of so many media players also ensures plurality, diversity and alternate channels of information and, therefore, differing opinions and dissenting views can no longer be suppressed. To that extent these media institutions have made a distinct contribution to democratising the information process and making available to the viewers a number of perspectives and experiences.

REFERENCES

David Miller (2004), (ed) *Tell me Lies : Propaganda and Media Distortion in the Attack on Iraq*. Pluto Press, London.

Donald Read (1992), *The Power of News* : The History of Reuters. Oxford University Press.

Kingsnorth Paul, (2003), *One No, Many Yeses, : A Journey to the Heart of the Global Resistance Movement,* Simon and Schuster UK Ltd, London.

Time (2003) *The BEEB takes on the world :* The BEEB worldwide How the best known public broadcaster learned to love capitalism.

6

INTELLECTUAL PROPERTY RIGHTS

In this era of globalisation and digital technologies, we find ourselves confronted with relatively new subjects which have become quite important for our understanding of contemporary economic and cultural scenario. One such subject is Intellectual Property Rights (IPRs), which plays a significant role in globalised industrial economy of which TRIPs (Trade-Related Aspects of Intellectual Property Rights) constitutes an important segment. TRIPs, in fact has become quite contentious for the developing countries, because it mostly benefits technologically advanced countries who wish to have open access to the markets of developing countries.

The agreement on TRIPs is one of the pillars of the Uruguay Round agreements and tightens intellectual property rights protection for the creator. The negotiations of the Uruguay Round (which took its name from its 1986 start in Uruguay) constitute a watershed in creating an enforceable global standard by linking IPRs with trade, making them binding through the World Trade Organization (WTO) process, which was created on 1 January 1995.

In the context of media industries it is interesting to note that whereas in the traditional status which television enjoyed as a cultural form, it had been protected from market forces because its services were captured by 'Public Service Broadcasting', but in the commercially traded terms, its status has been changed from culture to commodity.

This suits the American interests because in 1994, cultural industries in USA of which television and films are the major part constituted second only to the aerospace industry in terms of their contribution to American exports.

For countries like India where issues concerning agriculture, plant protection, biodiversity and traditional knowledge are important, an understanding of terms associated with IPRs is an absolute must.

For a better understanding of important terms, the IPRs, and their main forms—patents, copyright, trade marks and designs, are defined as under :

INTELLECTUAL PROPERTY

Intellectual property, often known as IP, allows people to own their creativity and innovation in the same way that they can own physical property. The owner of IP can control and be rewarded for its use, and this encourages further innovation and creativity to the benefit of us all.

In some cases IP gives rise to protection for ideas but in other areas there will have to be more elaboration of an idea before protection can arise. It will often not be possible to protect IP and gain IP rights (or IPRs) unless they have been applied for and granted, but some IP protection such as copyright arises automatically, without any registration, as soon as there is a record in some form of what has been created.

The four main types of IP are:

- *patents* for inventions—new and improved products and processes that are capable of industrial application;
- *trade marks* for brand identity—of goods and services allowing distinctions to be made between different traders;
- *designs* for product appearance—of the whole or a part of a product resulting from the features of, in particular, the lines, contours, colours, shape, texture or materials of the product itself or its ornamentation;
- *copyright* for material—literary and artistic material, music, films, sound recordings and broadcasts, including software and multimedia.

However, IP is much broader than this extending to trade secrets, plant varieties, geographical indications, performers rights and so on. To understand exactly what can be protected by IP, one will need to check the four main areas of *copyright, designs, patents* and *trademarks.* Often, more than one type of IP may apply to the same creation.

Patent

A patent gives an inventor the right for a limited period to stop others from making, using or selling an invention without the permission of the inventor.

Patents are about functional and technical aspects of products and processes, and specific conditions must be fulfilled to get a patent.

Most patents are for incremental improvements in known technology – evolution rather than revolution. The technology does not have to be complex.

Patent rights are territorial; for example a UK patent does not give rights outside of the UK. Some patents, such as those for medicinal products, may be eligible for a further 5 years protection with a Supplementary Protection Certificate.

Although there are potential pitfalls with patents, a patent can be of value to an inventor, and can also benefit other people. Arrangements can be made, through a licence or sale to use another inventor's patent. Additionally, large amounts of information can be learnt from other peoples' patents.

If someone makes, uses or sells the invention defined in the claims of your granted patent without your permission, what they are doing is known as "infringing" your patent.

If you become aware of infringement of your patent, you should consult a professional such as a Chartered Patent Agent.

As a first step, your professional advisor will probably prepare a carefully worded letter asking the infringer if they are aware of your patent.

This is because it is an offence to make groundless threats about infringement, which could undermine your case against the potential infringer. Often the mere existence of a patent is enough to deter a potential infringer. If not, legal action may be taken and damages claimed.

Trade mark

A trade mark is any sign which can distinguish the goods and services of one trader from those of another.

A sign includes words, logos, colours, slogans, three-dimensional shapes and sometimes sounds and gestures.

A trade mark is therefore a "badge" of trade origin. It is used as a marketing tool so that customers can recognise the product of a particular trader. It must also be capable of being represented graphically, that is, in words and/or pictures.

Design

A design refers to the appearance of the whole or a part of a product resulting from the features of, in particular, the lines, contours, colours, shape, texture or materials of the product or its ornamentation.

Designs are protected by three legal rights:

- registered designs
- unregistered design right, and
- artistic copyright

Design registration gives the owner a monopoly on their product design, i.e. the right for a limited period to stop others from making, using or selling a product to which the design has been applied, or in which it has been incorporated, without their permission and is additional to any design right or copyright protection that may exist automatically in the design.

Protection under Copyright

Copyright gives rights to the creators of the following kinds of material or "works":

- original literary works—for example: novels, newspaper articles, lyrics for songs, and instruction manuals. Computer programmes are also a form of literary work protected by copyright, as are some types of *databases*,

- original dramatic works, including works of dance or mime,
- original musical works,
- original artistic works—for example: paintings, drawings, engravings, sculptures, photographs, diagrams, maps, works of architecture and works of artistic craftsmanship,
- published editions of literary, dramatic or musical works. Protection in this case is of the typographical arrangement of the edition,
- sound recordings, in any form (e.g. tape or compact disc) – they can be recordings of other copyright works, such as music or literature, or other sounds,
- films, including videos and digital versatile discs (DVDs),
- broadcasts, which may be transmitted by cable or wireless means and including satellite broadcasts, but excluding most transmissions on the Internet.

Copyright does not protect *ideas, names or titles,* or functional or industrial articles.

An original work

A work can only be original if it is the result of independent creative effort. It will not be original if it has been copied from something that already exists. If it is similar to something that already exists but there has been no copying from the existing work either directly or indirectly, then it may be original.

The term "original" also involves a test of substantiality - literary, dramatic, musical and artistic works will not be original if there has not been sufficient skill and labour expended in their creation. But, sometimes significant investment of resources without significant intellectual input can still count as sufficient skill and labour.

Ultimately, only the courts can decide whether something is original, but there is much case law indicating, for example, that names and titles do not have sufficient substantiality to be original and that, where an existing work is widely known, it will be difficult to convince a court that there has been no copying if your work is very similar or identical.

Sound recordings, films and published editions do not have to be original but they will not be new copyright works if they have been copied from existing sound recordings, films and published editions.

Broadcasts do not have to be original, but there will be no copyright, if, or to the extent that, they infringe copyright in another broadcast.

Source – www.intellectual-property.gov.uk

The college and university students, faculty and scholars are face to face, almost everyday, with the issues of using copyright material in their research, studies and teaching work. Whereas several organisations and publishers are quite liberal in permitting the use of their work for research and teaching purposes; others are not. An understanding of their terms would help the users of copyright material about such limitations. Several universities have brought out guidelines for its students and staff. The guidelines developed by the Lancaster University are given below for two reasons :—

1. These guidelines will help further elucidating some of the terms elaborated earlier, and
2. Introduce the students with concepts like Fair Dealing and Copyright Licensing Agency.

Additionally, the author hopes that in India also the universitites and institutes of higher learning will initiate such guidelines for their students and staff.

Guidance for Students

Some guidelines excerpted from http://libweb.lancs.ac.uk are as under:

> Copyright is a form of intellectual property and, as the name suggests, it is a right and one which is implicit in the very act of creating anything which is original, be it a literary work, painting, sculpture, computer programme or just about anything which has a physical form of

expression. Unlike most rights however copyright can be waived or assigned to another person. Copyright does not have to be registered or proved, as long as the work is original, copyright is already invested in it automatically under law.

The typical length of time that a work is in copyright is 70 years from the end of the year in which the author died. A publisher will also have a copyright in the typographical arrangement of a literary work, typically 25 years from the date of publication. However, this period of time can vary with some kinds of material e.g. photographs and sound recordings, so advice should be sought if you are unclear.

It may come as some surprise that the very act of copying is almost always unlawful, unless it is covered by a statutory exception, such as the "fair dealing" clause or unless. the copyright owner has given permission, or unless it is done in accordance with a licensing scheme.

Fair Dealing

The CDPA (Copyright, Designs and Patents Act 1988) makes an allowance through the "fair dealing" clause for individuals to lawfully make copies of copyright material under certain circumstances. Fair dealing is not defined in the CDPA but this definition issued by the Copyright Licensing Agency is widely accepted:

- with a literary, dramatic, musical or artistic work is permitted if the copy is for the purposes of non-commercial research or private study. However, if the copying is carried out by a person other than the researcher or student himself/herself, then the person making the copy must know or have reason to believe that it will not result in copies of substantially the same material being provided to more than one person at substantially the same time and for substantially the same purpose.
- with the typographical arrangement of a published edition is permitted.

- with a work for the purpose of criticism or review, of that or another work or of a performance of a work, does not infringe any copyright in the work provided that it is accompanied by a sufficient acknowledgement, and provided that the work has been made available to the public.
- with a work (other than a photograph) for the purpose of reporting current events is permitted, provided again that it is accompanied by a sufficient acknowledgement.
- Copying for instructional use is permitted provided that it is done by an instructor or student and is not by reprography (e.g. photocopy, fax, etc.).
- Copying for examination purposes is allowed by reprography, provided this is not for a musical work.
- Copying with the copyright owner's permission is allowed.
- Copying in accordance with a licensing scheme is allowed.

The Copyright Licensing Agency

To deliver many of its courses, the University needs to be able to photocopy extracts from books and journals and distribute them to students. This activity falls outside the provisions of the CDPA for "fair dealing" hence the need to enter into an agreement with a body that represents the interests of authors and publishers, in this case the Copyright Licensing Agency, where you may find useful information to supplement this guide.

The University (along with all other Universities) has signed an agreement with the CLA which allows students and staff to lawfully make copies of printed materials, subject to strict limitations as defined below.

It should be noted that the CDPA nowhere states how much one may copy under fair dealing. This has been left for the courts to decide, but various organisations have issued guidelines which can help individuals make a judgement as to what is 'fair'.

The following limitations apply to copying generally:

- No more than one chapter from a book, or one article from a journal/periodical, or one single case report from a Law Report, or no more than 5 per cent of a given work, whichever is the greater.
- A poem, short story or short literary work is regarded as a 'work' in itself, and may not be copied in its entirety under Section 29 of the Act, but may be copied under the Licence as long as a maximum of ten pages is not exceeded.
- Criticism or review
  Prose works: One extract of no more than 400 words. Several extracts of no more than 300 words and totalling no more than 800 words.
  Poems: Up to 40 lines from a poem, provided that this extract amounted to no more than one quarter of the poem.

Some publishers have chosen not to allow the CLA to act as their agent in supplying permission to copy some or all of their works. These publishers will have to be approached direct. Also, several categories of publication, such as printed music, newspapers, maps, separate photographs and illustrations, industrial house journals etc. are not covered by the licence, including works published outside the countries listed on the Excluded Works List.

Copyright and your thesis

A thesis is created as part of the system of examination in being awarded a PhD. Under the regulations regarding educational copying you may include copyright material in your thesis upto the limits given above for fair dealing. The only problem you are likely to face is if your thesis is subsequently published, and you have included photographs or other artistic works such as diagrams, advertisements etc., and then you will have to obtain permission from the copyright owners to include those works.

Slides

There is no statutory provision for copying illustrations or diagrams from books, journals, etc. in copyright. Slides may be made from such illustrations for research or private study only (fair dealing) or with the permission of the copyright owner. This situation may change soon as the CLA is now making arrangements for the separate licensing of artistic works.

Non-copyright material

There will be occasions when you will not need to approach the CLA for copyright clearance. Apart from the obvious circumstance where copyright has expired there are some types of material which are in the "public domain" and can thus be freely copied as long as the source is acknowledged.

The CLA licence also covers government publications from foreign countries that are named in the licence, although the USA has long had a policy that most government publications are in the public domain.

Some non-governmental organisations, such as the United Nations, also have generous attitudes to the copying of their publications for educational purposes. Some journals also waive copyright for multiple copying for educational purposes.

> [*Note:* This needs to be explicitly stated on the journal itself or permission needs to be given to you in writing, as a verbal assurance by an editor or publisher would not be proof enough if challenged].

The publisher Blackwells has, for example, given permission for their journals to be freely copied for coursepack purposes—but this only applies to journals for which the Library already has a subscription.

Digitising texts

The scanning or digitisation of a copyright work is an act that is restricted by copyright because it involves the copying and electronic storage of a work. Some aspects of this area of the law are ambiguous. The best course of action is to obtain, in advance, written permission from the copyright owner to scan or digitise a work—such as a journal article. Or check the publication for any advice or statement on scanning and digitisation—although such statements are the exception rather than the rule.

However, it may be permissible to scan a single work for the purposes of personal research or private study. To make such a copy may be defensible under the Act's fair dealing defence for research or private study. But you should note the following points:

- a scanned or digitised copy should not be altered, edited, incorporated or changed in any way,
- a scanned or digitised copy should not be further forwarded by email, placed on an Intranet or Internet site, posted on a discussion group or used in any similar fashion without the prior express written permission of the copyright owner, or where it can be demonstrated that a licence specifically permits this. You should be able to produce such authorisation on request.
- preferably, a scanned or digitised copy should be stored on a non-networked drive—such as the C:\ drive of a PC. Networked storage is insecure and implicitly involves sharing, undermining the idea of individual use of the work.
- any scanning should conform to the limits set out in the section above—e.g. never more than one article from a single issue of a journal.
- single photographs, illustrations, charts, maps etc. should not be scanned at all (unless you are the copyright owner or have prior permission), nor should such material be isolated from a work and scanned in isolation
- It is usually also OK to take a single printout from the scanned document for your own private study or research.

BUILDING SAFEGUARDS INTO TRIPs AGREEMENT

Intellectual property rights manage two conflicting social concerns. One is protecting the rights of creators of technology by restricting conditions of diffusion for commercial use. The other is permitting open access to and sharing of scientific progress.

Are Society's Interests—the rights to health and the rights of indigenous peoples—adequately protected?

- *Access to health care* : Provisions restrain many public policies that promote wider access to health care. National laws of many developing countries have intentionally excluded pharmaceuticals from product patent protection (allowing only process patents) to promote local manufacturing capacity for generic drugs and to make drugs available at lower prices. The move from process to product patents introduced under the TRIPs agreement dramatically reduces the possibilities for local companies to produce cheaper versions of important life-saving drugs, such as those for cancer and HIV/AIDS. Local production in India had kept prices at a fraction of the levels in neighbouring countries. For example, in 1998 the anti-AIDS drug flucanazole cost $55 in India for 100 tablets (150 milligrams) but $697 in Malaysia, $703 in Indonesia and $817 in the Philippines.
- *Traditional knowledge and resource rights of indigenous peoples* : Biotechnology for plant breeding and pharmaceuticals has given enormous economic value to genetic materials, plant varieties and other biological resources. Life forms—plants and animals—have traditionally been excluded from patents. But the TRIPs agreement requires all WTO member countries to permit patents on micro-organisms and microbiological and non-biological processes. So "bioprospecting" has mushroomed—with scientists "reinventing" and patenting products and processes using traditional knowledge that communities have held for centuries.

> Patents have been awarded for using the healing properties of turmeric, for the pesticide properties of the *neem* tree and other plant properties—all part of traditional knowledge. In a number of such cases the patents were challenged and reversed.

The TRIPs agreement benefits technologically advanced countries. It is estimated that industrialized countries hold 97 per cent of all patents, and global corporations 90 per cent of all technology and product patents. Developing countries have little to gain from the stronger patent protection from the TRIPs agreement because they have little research and development capacity. Research and development for a new drug is estimated to cost around $150-200 million, but no developing country has a pharmaceutical sales volume of even $400 million. There is little evidence so far that patent protection has stimulated research and development in or for poor countries or that it offers the potential to do so.

TRIPS AGREEMENT AND HUMAN RIGHTS LAW

There are also questions about the compatibility of the TRIPs agreement with human rights law and environmental agreements. The Universal Declaration of Human Rights, the International Covenant on Economic, Social and Cultural Rights and the International Covenant on Civil and Political Rights recognize the human right to share in scientific progress. The Convention on Biodiversity requires states to protect and promote the rights of communities, farmers and indigenous peoples in their use of biological resources and knowledge systems. It also requires equitable sharing of the benefits arising from the commercial use of communities' biological resources and local knowledge.

Stronger human rights safeguards can be built into the TRIPs agreement and its implementation. The African Group of WTO members has proposed a review of the agreement, particularly for provisions to protect indigenous knowledge. India has suggested amendments to promote transfer of environmentally sound technology.

Stronger national policies are needed to protect society's interests within the realities of the new global regime. Compulsory licensing and parallel imports, provided for under the TRIPs agreement, can make essential medicines more affordable. They should be built into national legislation, as Argentina, India, South Africa and Thailand have done. Indigenous knowledge can be protected by such means as national gene banks and regulation of exports of germ plasm, as India is doing.

Source : Human Development Report 2000.

The current issues Indian Journal on Rural Development, *Kurukeshtra* (Vol. 52, No. 6) is primarily concerned with Intellectual Property Rights and Rural India. It brings forth the imperative need to be vigilant and wide awake about the rights which may accrue to the rural population by getting copyrights, patents and trademarks protected under the IPR legislation at the international level and documenting traditional knowledge available in India.

Almost all major stores in UK including Tesco and Alder stock *Basmati* rice, and Assam and Darjeeling Tea. For these products the place of origin itself is an indication of quality. Ayurvedic medicines, Yoga practices and several Indian herbs are being commercially marketed in large quantities. Their trade marks and patents need to be protected at the international level. This, however, can be done only if these get protection in the domestic market first.

In one of the articles—Trade Related Aspects of Intellectual Property Rights in *Kurukeshtra* gives quite useful information as under :—

Plant Varieties Protection

Biological forms were earlier considered sacrosanct, creation of the Supreme Being, beyond the limits of valuation or pricing carrying intrinsic values associated with it. But the wide ranging industrial application of biological technologies especially in pharmaceutical sectors, food processing and agriculture lead to the protection of biological process. The general principle governing grant of protection to new plant varieties is their novelty, distinctiveness, homogeneity, stability and repeatability.

Biodiversity

Concerns have been expressed in many quarters that the introduction of IPRs in agriculture may lead to erosion of biological diversity of cultivated plant species. The countries in the South are rich in biodiversity and majority of these countries depend on the diversified plant and animals to meet their nutritional and energy needs.

Traditional Knowledge

India is rich in traditional knowledge. However it has to do all it can to document and digitise, according to WTO format, all its traditional knowledge so that it can successfully face the type of situation it was confronted with in cases of *Neem* and *Basmati* rice. These efforts call for documenting the traditional knowledge inherited by the generations orally. It calls for codification of traditional knowledge and biodiversity. Now a project has been undertaken due to the collaborative efforts of the Indian National Institute of Science Communication (NISCOM) and the Department of Indian System of Medicine and Homoeopathy, following the successful Indian challenge of the turmeric and basmati patents granted by the US Patent Office in 1999.

Global technology could have a huge impact on poverty eradication by giving poor people access to seeds for high yielding food crops or to life saving medicines. However the 1994 TRIPs agreement tightens patent and copyright protection, favouring those who develop and market technology rather than looking after the society's interest in the diffusion of that technology.

The WTO conferences where TRIPs are negotiated are becoming more complex where developing countries generally lose out to the developed countries because of the latter's stronger bargaining power in terms of technology, resources and capacity to influence the decisions their own way. It is therefore essential that the developing counties pay attention to the following issues :

1. What are the potential benefits of the legislation on growth and equity.
2. What are the safeguards against negative impact on human rights.
3. Is the agreement consistent with the obligations under international human rights laws?

The emerging issues in the international intellectual property laws are becoming important for developing countries and more so for countries like India, who have to protect their traditional forms of knowledge, rich biodiversity, folk performances of its artists, and the products and the processes used in the traditional households. Developing countreis have been rather late in getting through the implications of the WTO regulations and agreements. In the globalised environment of trade, technology and communication, an understanding of IPRs has become a basic essential. The earlier we realise this, we will be in a better position to face the challenges.

The sheer opportunistic exploitation of the resources of the Third World countries by USA has not gone unnoticed by the writers and intellectuals in USA itself. In this context here is a short excerpt from a contribution by Adam Hochschild, and author of five books—in the magazine *Granta* (84, Winter 2003)

> I had not thought much about globalization until my wife and I lived for six months in India in the late 1990s. To read even India's mainstream newspapers was a revelation. Indians were outraged by American corporate attempts to patent basmati rice and a medicinal extract of the neem tree, products that Indians had been using for centuries. The local press abundantly covered an agreement then being signed, urged on the rest of the world by the United States and Europe, regarding free trade in 'financial services'. Under it American banks,

insurance companies, investment firms and the like can now get access to customers in countries like India while their Indian counterparts, of course, can in theory have equal access to the market. Guess which country's companies have the capital and infrastructure to come out ahead?

So it is not only the media imperialism, but it is the cultural, economic and trade hegemony of USA that the developing countries are confronted with. Saner elements in the American press themselves are critical of the attempts of the present US government to, 'rearrange the world to its own satisfaction.' The IPRs should not be allowed to be used for dominating the developing countries.

REFERENCES

Human Development Report 2000. UNDP, New York.

Kurukeshtra, (Vol. 52, No. 4) Ministry of Rural Development, New Delhi.

Websites : http://www.wipo.int.

http://www.intellectual_property.gov.uk

http://libweb.lancs.ac.uk

7

UNIVERSAL DECLARATION OF HUMAN RIGHTS AND RIGHT TO COMMUNICATION

Human rights constitute a precious heritage for the mankind for which many battles have been fought and won. And that battle continues in order to safeguard various freedoms: Freedom of Speech, Assembly and Religion; Freedom of the Press, Equal Protection under the Law and Freedom From Search and Seizure—all these freedoms have been enlisted in the essay—Certain Unalienable Rights, in a remarkable book : *Issues and Themes : Essays in American History and Civilization* brought out as a part of American Revolution Bicentennial 1776-1976.

I am referring to the above essay because of two reasons: Firstly, in the Declaration of American Independence (1776) Thomas Jefferson said:

> We hold these truths to be self evident, that all men are created equal, that they are endowed by their Creator with certain Unalienable Rights, that among these are life, liberty and the pursuit of Happiness.

Secondly, the protest to uphold Freedom from Search and Seizure has contemporary relevance—since search and seizure exercise carried on by police in USA, UK and several other European countreis in the wake of terrorist threat has alienated a large section of population in these countries. And of course struggle for the freedom of the press and violence against journalists continues at the same time. In fact large scale violence against journalists during War in Iraq and the murder of Forbes Russia editor Paul Klebnikov in July 2004 have been subjects of extensive press coverage in the international media.

The chapter discusses Universal Declaration of Human Rights, Communication as a Human Right and violence against media persons.

Human rights, as the term most commonly used, are the rights which every human being is entitled to enjoy and to have protected. The underlying idea of such rights, which are fundamental to human dignity—is that these rights be respected in the treatment of all men, women and children. These rights exist in some form in all cultures and societies. Human rights have been legally granted to the citizens of countries all over the world. These in general terms pertain to a decent life, protection from ill health and unemployment, freedom of expression, right to education and many other rights. The urge to freedom was enshrined first in the American Declaration of Independence, 1776. The French Declaration of Rights of Man and the Citizen and the American Bill of Rights were among the first historic initiatives to include human rights.

GLOBAL STRUGGLE FOR HUMAN RIGHTS

The concept of human rights evolved over a long period of history. Rights as instrument for limiting the use of autocratic power; only within states, and had no international application. Even within states, the concept tended to be confined to the rights of the upper strata of society, and a long time elapsed before it extended to all human beings without distinction of class or creed.

The famous Magna Carta of the thirteenth century represented an agreement between the king and the baronage, and although it contained a few clauses of general application, its main purpose was to protect the rights and privileges of the feudal lords of Britain. A much wider extension of the concept of human rights was brought about by the British revolutionaries who, after deposing and executing their king, laid down in the Bill of Rights of 1689 the minimum liberties to which all citizens were entitled. Nearly a century later, in 1776, the American revolutionaries after throwing off the yoke of the British King embodied in their Declaration of Independence the 'inalienable' human rights, which have been referred to earlier in the chapter. Shortly thereafter, the French revolutionaries, on deposing and executing their king, made the Declaration "men are born and remain free and equal in rights" and that purpose of any political association was the confirmation of the human rights of "liberty, property, security and resistance to oppression". Thus the concept of human rights has been all along a revolutionary concept.

The Charter of the United Nations which was adopted after the war by the San Francisco Conference gave prominence to the aim of promoting human rights and freedom. In the preamble of the Charter it was proclaimed : "We the peoples of the United Nations, determined..... to reaffirm faith in fundamental human rights, in the dignity and worth of the human person, in the equal rights of men and women and of nations large and small... have resolved to combine our efforts to accomplish these aims." In the very first article of the Charter, one of the declared purposes of the United Nations was stated to be the achievement of international cooperation in promoting and encouraging respect for human rights, the other purposes being the maintenance of internal peace and the development of friendly relations among nations.

UNIVERSAL DECLARATION OF HUMAN RIGHTS

The universal declaration of human rights was adopted by the general assembly "as a common standard of achievement for all peoples and all nations." Serious doubts were initially entertained about the practical value of the declaration even by people who appreciated the basic importance of human rights. These doubts must have been resolved by the experience of the last twenty-two years. Time and again the principles laid down in the declaration have been invoked and acted upon by the general assembly and other organs of the United Nations.

The rival principle of "domestic jurisdiction" did not prevent the general assembly from interfering or trying to interfere in cases where human rights were blatantly violated. This is well illustrated by the treatment given by the general assembly to the policy of apartheid pursued by the government of South Africa. By now the declaration has acquired a degree of practical authority, which had led some people to believe that it has virtually become a part of international law.

The contemporary international statement of these rights is the Universal Declaration of Human Rights which was adopted on 10 December 1948. The Declaration proclaims economic, social and cultural rights in addition to political and civil rights and freedom for the people of the world. These rights are considered the foundation of freedom, peace and justice in the world. Through this Declaration, the United Nations reaffirmed its faith in the worth of human beings and in the equal rights for men and women, and expressed determination to promote social progress and better standards of living of the large majority of the people.

Basic Principles

Some of the important basic principles of the Universal Declaration of Human Rights are :

1. All human beings are born free and equal in dignity and rights. They are endowed with reason and conscience and should act towards one another in a spirit of brotherhood.
2. Everyone is entitled to all the rights and freedoms set forth in this Declaration, without distinction of any kind, such as race, colour, sex, language, religion, political or other opinion, national or social origin.
3. Everyone has the right to life, liberty and security of person.
4. No one shall be held in slavery or servitude; slavery and the slave trade shall be prohibited in all their forms.

5. No one shall be subjected to torture or to cruel, inhuman or degrading treatment or punishment.
6. Everyone has the right to recognition everywhere as a person before the law.
7. All are equal before the law and are entitled without any discrimination to equal protection of the law. All are entitled to equal protection against any discrimination in violation of this declaration and against any incitement to such discrimination.

The major advances in human rights and human development came after the horrors of the Second World War. The 1945 Charter of the United Nations, followed by the Universal Declaration of Human Rights in 1948, ushered in a new era of international commitment to human freedoms :

1. Emphasizing the universality of rights, centred on the equality of all people.
2. Recognizing the realization of human rights as a collective goal of humanity.
3. Identifying a comprehensive range of all rights—civil, political, economic, social and cultural—for all people.
4. Creating an international system for promoting the realization of human rights with institutions to set standards, establish international laws and monitor performance (but without powers of enforcement).
5. Establishing the state's accountability for its human rights obligations and commitments under international law.

Work on international human rights legislation also continued. But polarized by the cold war, the rhetoric of human rights was reduced to a weapon in the propaganda for geopolitical interests. The west emphasized civil and political rights, pointing the finger at socialist countries for denying these rights. The socialist, and many developing countries, emphasized economic and social rights, criticizing the richest western countries for their failure to secure these rights for all citizens. In the 1960s this led to two separate covenants—one for civil and political rights, and the other for economic, social and cultural rights.

According to a well known analyst of international relations : "No other act of the United Nations has had anything like the same impact on the thinking of our times, the best aspirations of which it incorporates and proclaims. It may well be that it will live in history chiefly as a statement of great moral principle. As such its influence is deeper and more lasting than any political document or legal instrument."

Civil and Political Rights, Economic, Social and Cultural Rights

The Declaration covers two broad sets of rights. One set is known as Civil and Political Rights. The other set of rights is known as Economic, Social and Cultural Rights. In the words of the Declaration, these two sets of rights aim to give all people 'freedom from fear and want'. Both sets of rights must be protected as the 'foundation of freedom, justice and peace in the world'.

It is the responsibility of governments to protect the human rights proclaimed by the Declaration. Under the heading of Civil and Political Rights, all governments are to protect the life, liberty and security of their citizens. They should guarantee that no one is enslaved and that no one is subjected to arbitrary arrest and detention or to torture. Everyone is entitled to a fair trial. The right to freedom of thought, conscience and religion and to freedom of expression is to be protected.

Under the heading of Economic, Social and Cultural Rights, all governments are expected to try progressively to improve the living conditions for their citizens. For example, they should try to guarantee the right to food, clothing, housing and medical care, the pretection of the family and the right to social security, education and employment. They are to promote these rights without discrimination of any kind.

Several governments, however, as well as the news media, have come to use the term 'human rights' in a very narrow sense, referring only to the Civil and Political Rights set out in the Declaration. As a result the term 'human rights' is often broadly misused to mean only Civil and Political Rights and to exclude from considerations as a matter of rights, fundamental issues such as the right to food, health, education and social security.

The conventional wisdom had been that human rights were 'indivisible', meaning that respect for Civil and Political Rights could not be divorced from the enjoyment of Economic, Social and Cultural Rights. Expressed the other way round, authentic economic and social development could not exist without the political freedom to participate in the process, including the freedom to dissent.

Right to Development

'The right to development' was elaborated in the 1986 General Assembly Declaration on the Right to Development. It emphasizes the importance of Economic, Social and Cultural Rights and establishes that achieving these both is an individual and a collective effort.

The World Conference of Human Rights held at Vienna in June 1993 in its Final Declaration said : 'The universal nature of these rights is beyond question.' The entire spectrum of human rights was endorsed, without division. 'All human rights are universal, indivisible, and interdependent and interrelated.'

The Way Forward

The World Conference affirmed an affirmative action plan to implement the Declaration. Some of the important goals set for the future are :

- The full range of human rights must be respected as the equal and inalienable birthright of all people. All people, regardless of their characteristics or social situation, must be understood to have the same fundamental rights. No one is to fall, at any time or for any reason, outside the circle of those whose rights are to be universally protected.

- The achievement of development and democracy must be based on universal respect for human rights and fundamental freedoms. This is essential if people are to determine their own political, economic, social and cultural destinies and to participate fully in their societies. This applies to all people and all societies and must be understood to embrace individuals and groups thus far excluded from the free and equal expression of human rights.
- The promotion and protection of economic, social and cultural rights must become subject to the same scrutiny and enforcement which can already be applied to civil and political rights. The first need is for a system of indicators to measure progress in the realization of the rights set forth in the International Covenant on Economic, Social and Cultural Rights.
- Gross and systematic violations of civil and political rights are taking place on a vast scale. Every effort must be made to halt these abuses which include arbitrary detentions, torture, summary executions, and 'disappearances'. Every instance must be condemed and measures taken to end impugnity for those responsible.
- The protection of one of the rights must not be invoked as a justification for the denial or violation of other universally recognized rights. The promotion of social justice cannot be used to legitimize political persecution; nor may the rule of law be used as a basis for the perpetuation of economic injustice and social deprivation.
- Discrimination in all its forms must be eliminated, if people are to be able to exercise their inalienable rights and freedoms. Racism and racial discrimination, xenophobia and other forms of intolerance must be the target of major legislative and social programmes to

prevent these abuses, protect potential victims and create a global ethos of mutual respect between all members of the human family.

- The rights of women of all ages, which have been denied on a massive scale worldwide, must be accorded full respect. This is a fundamental building block in the protection of the fundamental rights of all people everywhere. Action in a wide range of fields—legislative, economic, social, and educational—is needed to halt all forms of violence against women and to curtail their exploitation and harassment.
- Every state must have an effective system for investigating and redressing violations of human rights. A strong and independent administration of justice must be secured in order to sustain human rights, democracy and development. Ratification of international human rights treaties by all governments is also an indispensable part of the process of establishing a universal rule of law in defence of human rights.
- The role of non-governmental organisations in the defence of human rights must be openly recognized and accepted. The harassment and brutal attacks to which human rights workers are often subjected must cease.

Third Generation of Human Rights

Human rights are indivisible, but they are also inseparable from the major aspirations of our time. It is, therefore, vital to foster constantly an awareness of the links uniting human rights, development, peace, disarmament and many other issues. This broad vision ties in with the thinking of those who call for all to urge the formulation of "third generation" of human rights. If the principles proclaimed by the American revolution (1776) and the French revolution (1789) defined the "first generation" human rights—civil and political rights, the October revolution (1917) gave rise to economic and social rights, which have been confirmed and enlarged by the different revolutionary movements during the twentieth century and which constitute the "second generation" rights. In certain international forums – there has been a strong view that "third generation" rights be enshrined as strongly as the earlier rights and implemented vigorously. These are : the right to development, the right to a healthy environment, the right to peace, the right of access to the common heritage of mankind – rights whose distinctive feature is that they all reflect a certain humane conception of life.

The arbitrary exercise of power has traditionally reinforced the helplessness of the powerless. When governments operated on the principle of the divine right of kings, rulers did not seek legitimacy for their power in any notion of justice. The struggle against such injustice demanded that social institutions be based on legitimacy, consent and rule of law. In the 21st century securing freedom against injustice will require institutions that protect people through transparent rules applied equally to all.

Human Rights and Partisan Politics

Quite often the issue of protection of human rights is raised as a part of on-going political and partisan propaganda. The United States has protested against the imprisonment without trial of dissidents and democracy proponents, and the use of prison and child labour in manufacturing and has insisted on improvements in the human rights record in China. It has attempted repeatedly, but unsuccessfully to gain censure for the Chinese human rights policies at the United Nations Commission on Human Rights. Prior to the return of Hong Kong to China, the US Congress passed legislation affirming the human rights of the people of Hong Kong.

The Chinese troops occupied Tibet in 1950 and have waged war on the Dalai Lama and the Tibetan Buddhism. The Dalai Lama has been seeking autonomy for Tibet since 1959 when he unsuccessfully tried to oust Chinese forces and was forced into exile into India. The Dalai Lama has proposed autonomy for Tibet while allowing China to retain control over defence and foreign affairs. The major concern has been the elimination of the Tibetan culture as more Chinese move into the region. The United States has protested against the treatment of the people and culture of China.

China, on the other hand, views this criticism as attacks on its sovereignty and interference in its internal matters. It does not accept the role of the United States as a global judge of human rights. China also considers it as a clash based on its cultural values. Chinese leaders place a higher premium on social order and lesser on individual suppression. China emphasises collective order whereas the Western cultures stress individual freedoms.

USA and Human Rights Violations

The United States, however, has come in for severe criticism in the context of human rights violations in Iraq. Almost all the mainstream newspapers in Britain—particularly *The Guardian*, and *The Independent*, extensively covered these practices in the Abu Ghraib prison in Iraq and Bagram in Afghanistan with detailed photographs and interviews with the detainees and their relations and friends, senior US military sources and human rights monitors. Even brief excerpts from these articles would show the strong revulsion that the publication of photographs of Iraqi prisoners being held by the leather strap leash, stripped and forced to perform sexual acts, has evoked.

The Destruction of Morality

> "The hooded man with the wires attached to his hands has now become an iconic portrait, every bit as memorable as the picture of the second aircraft flying into the World Trade Centre. No, of course, we haven't killed 3000 Iraqis. We have killed many more. And the same goes for Afghanistan.
>
> But in the history of the Middle East, these pictures already have the status of those most damaging snapshots of the Vietnam War: the police chief in Saigon executing

his Vietcong prisoners; the naked girl burnt by napalm, the pile of bodies at My Lai."

(From the frontpage news article by Robert Fisk in *The Independent*, 7 May 2004)

The Guardian ran a special report in its G_2 Supplement on 23 June 2004 – Inside America's secret Afghan gulag and earlier in the same supplement on 24 May 2004, 'The photos are US' – Real meaning of the Abu Ghraib pictures.

Sometimes readers are gripped by a feeling of helplessness: Is there no way to curb the excesses of the US forces indulging in open violation of human rights of prisoners and common citizens in both the countries. No, it seems the backlash has already begun. The continuing publication of pictures is being taken by many Americans as suggesting that they do not have the right to defend themselves.

Communication as Human Right

Article 19 of the Universal Declaration of Human Rights says : Everyone has the right to freedom of opinion and expression.

Article 19 of the Indian Constitution says much the same thing, guaranteeing for all citizens the right to freedom of speech, expression, conscience and religion. Freedom of speech and expression are basic rights in any democratic society. Democracy is based on the premise that every citizen has the right to express his or her views freely. This is the reason why no restrictions may be placed on public speeches, assemblies and group discussions where dissident opinions are expressed.

In democratic societies the same rights are extended to journalists. Such rights are at par – no more and no less – than the right to free speech extended to ordinary citizens. Since a journalist seeks information that might be withheld and also tries to bring such information alive, there is an inevitable conflict between the democratic requirements of an open society and the need to preserve official secrecy. Such secrecy is sought to be maintained in 'national interest', 'security of the state' and such other reasons. The press, on the other hand, sees itself as the conscience keeper and watchdog of society. It is charged with the responsibility of giving citizens the information they need to understand the policies and working of the government. This often leads to a clash of interests.

Another important reason to defend and protect right of information, and its communication, is that it can greatly reduce the incidence of human rights abuse by creating a climate in which people are enabled to protect themselves against official high handedness and improve their lives.

However communication rights remain for most of the journalists and people of the world only a vision and aspiration. The ground situation is quite different. That is why a leading media academic—Professor Cees Hamelink took a commendable initiative in organising World Forum on Communication Rights in December 2003 in Geneva. The Statement on Communication Rights is a valuable document and incorporates relevant references to communication rights in international human rights instruments. The Statement on Human Rights is given as an Annexure alongwith the Universal Declaration of Human Rights.

The World Forum on Communication Rights selected four main themes to illustrate the spectrum of communication rights and their interconnections. These were :—

Communication and Poverty : How poverty has 'disappeared' from media, the role of communication in development, and community-led access in poor areas.

Communication, Conflict and Peace : Drawing on experience and trends in media in the context of conflict—before, during and after; the militarisation of ICTs; censorship and surveillance.

Communication, Copyright, Patents and Trade : The impact of current and proposed regional and global trade agreements on media and culture; global consolidation of corporate media; copyright restrictions and alternatives, open source and free software.

Communication and Human Rights: Its role not only in freedom of expression and privacy, but in all human rights, from the right to a fair trial and freedom of movement, to freeom of assembly and workers' rights, together with democratic governance.

Let us hope the Forum makes rapid strides in creating awareness about Communication Rights and shows the media academics and practitioners the way to strengthen these rights.

Violence against Journalists

That journalists have often become targets, face physical danger in times of conflict and even otherwise while covering public demonstrations and meetings which are suppressed by the authority—is widely known. Amnesty International had recorded that in 1977, 104 correspondents were imprisoned or missing in 25 countries. The International Press Institute covering a period of 15 months in 1976-78, compiled the data as: 24 journalists murdered, 57 journalists, murdered, torturted or kidnapped. Foreign correspondents are known to have been expelled by the host governments for unfavourable reporting.

The MacBride Commission also discussed the question of affording protection to journalists and it stated: There seems to be a general consensus among the various organisations of journalists, broadcasters and publishers that some effective measures should be adopted to ensure better protection of journalists in the exercise of their profession in dangerous situations whether such situations arise in international or non-international armed conflicts.

There has been no satisfactory solution to the issue of protecting journalists in times of conflict. An article, Target the Media, published in *Tell me Lies,* by Tim Gopsill, lists 17 journalists including cameramen and translators who met their deaths in the 2003 Iraq war. These journalists came from different countries and belonged to different organisations and also included two embedded journalists who were protected by the army units.

The US Defence Secretary Donald Rumsfeld endorsed the policy of inducting embedded journalists in its military units. He called it as "his core principle." The editors fell for this proposal because it ensured the protection of their staff. The 'embeds' would be protected by the army units whereas their freewheeling colleagues, who were called "unilaterals" were not afforded any such protection.

There have been open allegations that the US troops targeted the journalists who were on their own or who were reporting independently particularly reporters from Al Jazeera.

The murder of Forbes Russia editor Paul Klebnikov in July 2004 shows that little has changed, reports *The Guardian* (14 July). In this context *New York Times* (13 July) *says*, "Twenty journalists have now been assassinated for their work; 14 since Vladimir Putin became President. Not one of the murders has been solved. *The Washington Post* of the same date said, "Those who killed Klebnikov are killing today, plan to kill tomorrow, and know they will roam free to kill for years to come."

Not a happy augury for journalists or the profession of journalism.

Protecting Human Rights

There are a large number of organisations working at the international level, at the level of national governments and in the non-governmental sector. There are also Human Rights Commissions and the judicial bodies enforcing human rights under the relevant laws passed by the legislatures and the parliaments.

The United Nations High Commissioner for Human Rights works for strengthening the UN Human rights programme and provides UN treaty monitoring bodies. It engages in dialogue with governments on human rights issues and provides advisory services and technical assistance when requested.

No discussion on human rights can be complete without a reference to Amnesty International and the World Social Forum.

Amnesty International

Amnesty International (AI) is a worldwide movement of people who campaign for internationally recognized human rights.

Through its members and allies, AI remains committed to revitalizing the vision of human rights as a powerful tool for achieving justice for all. AI's vision is of a world in which every person enjoys all of the human rights enshrined in the Universal Declaration of Human Rights and other international human rights standards. In pursuit of this vision, it undertakes research and action focused on preventing and ending grave abuses of the rights to physical and mental integrity, freedom of conscience and expression, and freedom from discrimination, within the context of its work to promote all human rights.

The Amnesty is independent of any government, political ideology, economic interest or religion. It does not support or oppose any government or political system, nor does it support or oppose the views of the victims whose rights it seeks to protect. It is concerned solely with the impartial protection of human rights. It has a varied network of members and supporters around the world. At the latest count, there were more than 1.8 million members, supporters and subscribers in over 150 countries and territories in every region of the world. Although they come from many different backgrounds and have widely different political and religious beliefs, they are united by a determination to work for a world where everyone enjoys human rights.

It is a democratic, self-governing movement. Major policy decisions are taken by an International Council made up of representatives from all national sections. AI's national sections and local volunteer groups are primarily responsible for funding the movement. No funds are sought or accepted from governments for AI's work investigating and campaigning against human rights violations.

The Amnesty International Report 2004 covers the human rights situation in 155 countries. The Report reflects those challenges. It documents the human rights situation in 155 countries and territories in 2003, and summarizes regional trends. It reports on areas of work being prioritized and developed by Amnesty International – such as violence against women; economic, social and cultural rights; and justice for refugees and migrants - and celebrates the achievements of activists in these and other areas.

The report says, "In a dangerous and divided world, it is more important than ever that the global human rights movement remains strong, relevant and vibrant".

WORLD SOCIAL FORUM - ANOTHER WORLD IS POSSIBLE

The World Social Forum is an open meeting place where groups and movements of civil society opposed to neo-liberalism and a world dominated by capital or by any form of imperialism, but engaged in building a planetary society centred on the human person, come together to pursue their thinking, to debate ideas democratically, to formulate proposals, share their experiences freely and network for effective action. The WSF proposes to debate alternative means to building a globalization in solidarity, which respects universal human rights and those of all men and women of all nations and the environment, and is grounded in democratic international systems and institutions at the service of social justice, equality and the sovereignty of peoples.

The two first editions of the World Social Forum were held in Porto Alegre, Brazil, on the same dates as the World Economic Forum was meeting in Davos. By proposing to strengthen an international coalition of the widest range of social movements and organizations, on the principle of respect for differences, autonomy of ideas and forms of endeavour, the WSF ceased to be a single locus of convergence for the struggle against neo-liberal globalization and sought to become a world process. The WSF has taken up a wider range of ideological and cultural positions including Global Justice Movement.

The World Social Forum is a world process. All the meetings that are held as part of this process have an international dimension. It brings together and interlinks only organizations and movements of civil society from all the countries in the world, but intends neither to be a body representing world civil society. The format of the programme is to provide a larger space for the self-organised activities of the groups.

Fourth World Social Forum Edition – Mumbai : During January 2004, the fourth WSF edition was held in Mumbai, India which also turned out to be a protest against the US domination of world policies and war in Iraq.

Thematic Areas and Sub-Areas for the discussion at forum were:

1. Militarism, War and Peace
2. Media, Information, Knowledge and Culture
3. Democracy, Ecological and Economic Security

 (i) Debt, finance and trade
 (ii) Land, Water and Food Sovereignty
 (iii) Labour and World of Work in Production and Social Reproduction
 (iv) Social sectors – food, health, education – and social security

4. Exclusions, Discrimination, Dignity, Rights and Equality

 (i) Nation, State, citizenship, law and justice
 (ii) Caste, race and other forms of descent/work based exclusions
 (iii) Religion, culture and identities
 (iv) Patriarchy, Gender and Sexuality

A short summary of the evaluation by Kamal Mitra Chenoy, Professor of international studies at Jawaharlal Nehru University, and a member of the India Organizing Committee, World Social Forum 2004, is as under:

The 2004 World Social Forum (WSF) was for the first time held in Mumbai (Bombay), India, between 16-21 January. More than 100,000 delegates came together for the biggest anti-neoliberal globalization meeting ever, representing trade unions, environment, women, human rights, peace, alternative sexuality and other movements.

Poor tribals, dalits [former untouchables], street vendors, daily wage workers, rural labourers and people displaced by large projects such as mega dams were also present in force. They came together in more than 1,200 seminars and workshops, while marches, rallies, street theatre, songs and other events continued well into the nights.

The forum's slogan—"another world is possible"—symbolizes both its rejection of globalization and the latter claim that it is the only alternative.

The Forum contends that, instead of ensuring even in the long run, equitable development, neoliberal globalization actually globalizes poverty and aggravates inequality and oppression. Globalization is not an alternative. Only a people-friendly, sustainable, egalitarian and secular development is possible. With the diversity and complexity of the world, no one alternative or model is feasible, which is why the discussion of many alternatives makes eminent sense. Looking to Europe, the WSF seeks allies—not only in like-minded movements but also in governments and the EU—to deal with such core issues as agricultural subsidies, intellectual property rights and trade-related investment measures. There is also a need to reform and reconsider the economic models presented by institutions such as the World Bank, the World Trade Organization and the International Monetary Fund—which are so unfriendly to the South.

The fact such issues were intensively debated by delegates from more than 90 countries and many political tendencies make the WSF much more representative than the World Economic Forum to which it is in fact a counterpoint. The activists and leaders represent the mass of their peoples and their aspirations far more than the finance ministers and CEOs that meet in Davos, representing the power and capital that dominates the world. The WSF is a significant effort to right this balance by facilitating dialogue and shared experience - and this was clear in Mumbai, where the poor and marginalized were present in depth.

In 2005, the WSF will take place in Porto Alegre, Rio Grande do Sul (Brazil).

REFERENCES

Human Rights, the New Consensus (1994) Regency Press in association with United Nations High Commission for Refugees, New York.

The Guardian (2004) G_2 Section, 23 June, London.

The Independent (2004), Destruction of Morality, 7 May, London.

UNDP (2000) Human Development Report, *Human Rights and Human Development*, Oxford University Press.

8

INDIA AND GLOBAL INFORMATION REVOLUTION

India—a country of sub-continental dimensions, with over a billion population presents a contrasting and unusual setting for a global information revolution.

Consider this : On 21 September 1995, it was widely reported in Delhi and other Indian cities that the Hindu deities were drinking milk. This unusual news event immediately disseminated world-wide and several million people, not only in India but throughout the world wherever the Indian diaspora lived, lined up to offer milk to the divine image. This news event was given a number of interpretations: the nature of global village and the wide distribution of individuals of Indian ancestry (Singhal and Rogers in their book—*India's Communication Revolution : From Bullock Carts to Cyber Marts).*

In his Reith Lectures on globalisation (earlier referred to in Chapter third), Anthony Giddens also mentions this episode in the chapter on tradition. Quoting Denis Vidal, an anthropologist who had commented on this phenomenon as under :

> By manifesting themselves simultaneously in every country of the world inhabited by Indians, the Hindu deities may have succeeded in performing the first ever miracle in tune with an era haunted by the slogan of globalisation.

Giddens said in the above case science had been enlisted in the service of faith.

The above two references make it clear that in a vast and ancient country like India science and faith co-exit; similarly it is also a country where bullock carts survive in the villages as a means of transport alongwith cyber cafes in the "global" and "informational" environment of international communication where the Indian scientists and technologists work to usher in IT culture. We shall have to keep both these contrasting aspects in mind, which impinge on our discussion on India and Global Information Revolution.

CULTURAL AND COMMUNICATION DIVERSITY

India, as is well known, is host to a staggering variety and richness of cultural and communication diversity. In the ancient Indian society, religious, philosophical and cultural discourse was characterised by oral communication. Cradle of an ancient civilisation, India has also been a rich repository of traditional forms of communication. For thousands of years Indian religious and social landscape was dotted with saints, scholars and wandering monks, priests and preachers who would move from one place to another and disseminate thoughts and ideas on various aspects of life, religion and social behaviour. Even today such congregations of men and women are frequently organised. In fact such programmes—religious, cultural and entertainment-oriented film-based functions—are organised even in foreign countries in which the Indian diaspora enthusiastically participates. This pattern of communication—oral, interpersonal, traditional aided by the gadgets of electronic technology—extensive public address system, closed circuit TV, recording for cable television for subsequent broadcasts and wider dissemination through audio and video modes—is a communication experience in itself. In India there is an explosion of both mass media—press, radio and television—and promising beginnings of the cyber media which has triggered an IT revolution in the country. Interestingly the emerging IT revolution in India also has its contradictions. While the country has several successful demonstrations of IT usage, the lag in IT penetration and effectiveness—as is seen from such indicators as low per capita telephone density, PCs and Internet hosts—brings it face-to-face with such situations as digital divide or e-exclusion.

Apart from all these issues impacting India's position in the global communication revolution in the 21 century, we shall also discuss India's contribution to promoting non-aligned news agency pool, the collaboration of Indian news agencies with international news agencies, India as a outsourcing destination of the world and finally the influence that the Indian diaspora enjoys at the international level.

INDIA's CONTRIBUTION TO NON-ALIGNED NEWS AGENCY POOL

The Non-Aligned News Agency Pool, (NANAP) is an arrangement for exchange of news among the agencies of the non-aligned countries who were for long victims of *imbalances and bias* in the flow of news. The pool came into existence in 1976 with India as its first chairman (1976-79). The Pool is a world-wide operation embracing four continents—Asia, Europe, Africa and Latin America and the Pool news is exchanged in four languages—English, French, Spanish and Arabic.

The activities of the Pool are coordinated by an elected body known as the Co-ordinating Committee with a chairman as its head. The Chairman and the members of the Co-ordinating Committee are elected by a General Conference, which is the top decision making body. Since the inception of the pool, six General Conferences, 17 regular meetings and one special meeting of the Co-ordinating Committee have taken place.

India has played a vital role in the creation and expansion of Pool. The Press Trust of India operates the India News Pool Desk. The agency receives news copy from the Pool partners and, in turn, contributes Indian news into the exchange arrangement. The incoming news traffic from the member agencies into PTI is over 20,000 words per day. The news is exchanged through a network of E-mail, satellite and terrestrial communication with links with other news agencies including

Antara (Indonesia), Bernama (Malaysia), BSS (Bangladesh) and ZANA (Zambia).

As a part of the News Pool operation, the Indian Institute of Mass Communication offers a regular diploma course in development journalism.

COLLABORATION WITH INTERNATIONAL NEWS AGENCIES

In the fast emerging global news environment, no news organisation can work in isolation. Arrangements for the exchange and dissemination of news form an essential part of the working of major news organisations throughout the world.

Whereas the PTI service is received by BBC, London, the PTI has arrangements with AP (Associated Press) and AFP (Agence France Presse) for distribution of their news in India. AP's photo and international commercial information are also distributed in the country through PTI. It has bilateral news exchange relations with several news agencies belonging to countries of Asia, Africa, Europe and Latin America.

Likewise the other major news agency—United News of India (UNI) distributes world news from Reuters, the world's largest information company and DPA, the German News Agency. It also has exchange arrangements with Xinhua of China, RIA Novosti of Russia and several other news agencies from countries in middle east, Asia and Africa. UNI distributes pictures from the French News Agency, AFP.

Besides collaboration with news agencies, international and national from different countries, both the Indian news agencies have correspondents in major cities of the world including Beijing, Bangkok, Colombo, Dhaka, Dubai, Islamabad, London, Moscow, New York and Washington.

Besides these two news agencies, All India Radio also maintains links between India and the rest of the world through its External Division. Through its external broadcasts, AIR aims to keep the overseas listeners in touch with the contemporary developments in the country through news, current affairs features and programmes on sports and literature. AIR has based its correspondents at Washington, Brussels, Dubai, Kathmandu, Dhaka, Colombo and Hongkong.

All these efforts are geared towards keeping the Indian audience posted with latest news and views from different countries. However with the onset of 24-hour news channels—rolling news, and the online news networks the media environment appears at times to be suffering from information overload. It seems to be the case of too many media players trying to seek the attention of the readers and viewers all at the same time because for them, besides being the consumers of their news and entertainment products, they are also the recipients of their advertising messages.

Whereas several of India's newspapers, like *The Hindu* and *The Times of India* are well known abroad for their quality coverage, India does not have a world class broadcasting service like BBC or a newspaper like *The Times*—the "modest journal" which began life as *The Daily Universal Register* in 1785 and celebrated its bicentenary as the best-known newspaper in the world.

INDIA's COMMUNICATION REVOLUTION

In 1989, the two senior media academics joined together as coauthors in writing a book—*India's Information Revolution.* One was Arvind Singhal, an Indian who earned his degree in Engineering from University of Delhi and studied in USA for his MA and Ph.D degrees and the other Everett Rogers, a US national who lived in India off and on over the past 36 years. Rogers was already a well known name for his studies on diffusion on agricultural innovations and was widely referred to by scholars in agricultural communication and extension education.

Both the academics again collaborated in writing another book in 2001 : *India's Communication Revolution – From Bullock Carts to Cyber marts.* A study of the both the books—which constitute an essential reading for the present author—show how far India has journeyed on path towards what the authors have termed as *informatization.* A reference from the Preface (p. 24) will elucidate the point further :

> Since our 1989 book, television audiences in India have multiplied four-fold, the number of telephones has increased six-fold, cable television—which was then almost non-existent in India—has reached 35 million homes, and Indian computer software exports have increased fifty-fold! ...... India has changed so much in the past decade that our present book represents a focus on the informatization path to development. This book is not first about Indians in India, it is also about Indians in Silicon Valley or wherever they are today in the Indian diaspora.

Today India has become the favoured destination for software outsource business and remote processing. A number of financial journals have described India as the 'back office of the world'—which essentially means outsourcing a wide range of office skills which richer economies are only too eager to outsource to India.

India—A destination for Software Outsourcing

During the 1990s India developed a dominant position in the software outsourcing business. The outsourcing business essentially means data entry and conversion, for example medical transcription; project design, website services and direct customer interaction. Some of the duties being assigned are :

Rule setting : Here a worker may decide, whether under an airlines rules a passenger qualifies for an upgrade.

Problem solving : Deciding if an insurance claim should be paid.

Knowledge Services : Requires specialists, engineers and lawyers using databases.

Data entry and conversion : Medical Transcription.

Several factors have contributed to India's dominant position in software outsourcing business :

- There is a huge pool of highly educated, English-speaking software workers in India who have the technical skills. This pool of Indian workers can be drawn upon flexibly to meet changes in staff requirements and skill shortages in contracting firms.
- Indian sub-contractors offer huge cost savings over United States levels, even allowing for some differences in productivity. The wage levels for US software workers during 1980s-1990s were between 6-8 times higher than those in India.
- The New Economic Policy – ushered in 1991 – opened India to foreign money flows and provided much greater role for private enterprise, streamlined government procedures and stimulated economic growth. The policy became increasingly liberal in attitudes towards foreign investments and also began offering a number of incentives to foreign investors.
- Indian companies are keen to enter into collaborations and alliances with western firms in order to gain access to overseas markets, technologies and opportunities to expand business.

The expansion in ICT services has been so fast, that NASSCOM, India's flag ship association of IT companies, estimates that India will employ 1.1 million people and earn $ 17 billion from IT enabled services by 2008.

No wonder, major international companies like GE Capital Services took initiative in opening India's first international call centre in mid 1990s. Other companies which operate major back-office facilities in India include British Airways, Swissair and American Express.

It is not only the IT industry, but the service sector as a whole that is growing rapidly. Media, advertising, personal financial and banking services, entertainment and leisure industry are expanding at a fast pace.

However India has started facing competition in its outsourcing work and it is no longer an unchallenged destination. In a business feature published in *The Guardian* (18 August 2004), it was written that Vietnam was fast becoming a major source for outsourcing work for big manufacturing companies like Honda, BMW and Mercedes Benz, which have already developed a significant presence there. The Managing Director of Harvey Nash's software development division—a London Stock Exchange listed company, Paul Smith says, "We chose not to go to India because although they were very good at doing volume copying of software they were not raising their quality and architecture." According to Mr. Smith Vietnam has the opportunity to overtake both India and China, as highly skilled English—speaking workforce emerges from Hanoi University.

INDIAN DIASPORA

At a time when countries all over the world are taking increasing note of the diaspora element in their population, the Indians overseas have also started identifying themselves as an influential group. Just as the Jewish and Irish diasporas in the United States influence American policies, Indian migrants wield enormous economic and political clout. An eminent economist Jagdish Bhagwati of Columbia University calls Indian-American 'as a highly successful, intellectually eminent and economically prominent group that has all the networking advantages that a merit-based immigration—oriented society such as the American society offers'.*

Referring to the dominant influence of the Indian migrants in Silicon Valley, Singhal and Rogers say: Silicon Valley has become a primary destination in recent years, with over 80,000 Indians working in this technopolis in 2000. In fact, Silicon Valley has become a kind of alumni club for India's IITs. At the Oracle Company's cafetaria in Silicon Valley, for example

* From *India's Communication Revolution – From Bullock Carts to Cyber Marts;* pages 150-151.

sambhaar-rice is a standard menu item. Indian restaurants, grocery stores, Hindu temples, Hindi movie houses and schools of Indian dance and music now dot the landscape of Silicon Valley.

During the Millennium Year 2000, *India Today* brought out The Millennium Series and its volume III was a collection of contributions brought out under the title *India Tomorrow*. An absolutely first rate collection of ideas, which the Editor-in-Chief of the India Today group, Aroon Purie calls as 'a touchstone for the future', the volume attracted ideas from futurologists, economists and politicians, scientists and space scientists, as also from thinktanks like Centre for Policy Research and Confedertion of Indian Industry. In the article—Money Matters—Tarun Das, Director General, Confederation of Indian Industry says: Information Technology is already reshaping the world's economies and has created a new powerhouse in India, especially in four southern states. The IT—related services have linked India with the US, Europe and Japan. IT is changing jobs, lives, opportunities—the future of a large body of people. It will do more. It is a little known fact that Uttar Pradesh—considered one of the most backward states—is today No. 4 in software exports. The same can happen anywhere. All you need is a computer and a telephone. Professor Michael Dertouzous of MIT has done some interesting research. He came to the CII earlier this year and presented a thesis, according to which India can earn $ 1 trillion (Rs. 46,00,000 crore) annually by providing e-services to the world, especially the U.S. And what is it that we need to earn this? The answer is so obvious, it is shocking: the ability to write and speak English. According to Dertouzous, India has 50 million people who do just that and their earning capacity is US $ 20,000 (Rs. 9.2 lakhs) per year. This make $ 1 trillion. The new ball game in the world is export of services from home base. And English is the key. Plus, of course, the telecom infrastructure.*

Likewise India's intertainment industry is likely to see a healthy growth of 20 per cent over the next few years because of rising global interest. According to a study conducted by

---

* *India Today*, Special Millennium Issue : October 2000 (p. 54).

CII, the Indian TV content producers have already made inroads into Asia-Pacific markets and there is a growing interest in broadcasters and distributors in the US and Britain to look at India-specific content. India is already a world leader in the cutting edge of e-cinema. Over 130 cinema theatres had already changed over from film, based systems and were exhibiting their fare using digital projectors backed by computer servers.

India's mobile phone market has grown rapidly in the last few years on the back of spiralling income levels and falling phone tarrifs and handset prices, making India one of the fastest growing markets.

The Celebration of India

When the British Indian Councillor's Association (BICA) asked me to speak on the occasion of 58th Anniversary of India's independence in Slough, a town just close to the Heathrow Airport, known for its multi-cultural, multilingual and multi-religious population; the ideas rushed through my mind as to the long road to progress that India has travelled and the place it has made for itself in the community of nations particularly in the fields of information technology and entertainment and the impact that the Indian cultural traditions had made worldwide. A brief summary of the speech, highlighting India's role in IT revolution illustrates some of the issues raised in the Chapter is as under:

In the summer of 2002, when London burst out in Bollywood colours, the world at large realised that, Indian music and dance, in all their splendour, Indian food, Indian writing and Indian cinema were successfully competing at the global level. With Ayurveda and yoga having already conquered the imagination of the western world, there has been no doubt amongst Indians – residents and non-residents – that the voice of India and its distinct sights and sounds were making an unprecedented impact.

Today the Indian diaspora has come of age, and unlike in the past, its negative images do not overshadow the positive. In USA, the Indian community's political influence is distinctly on the rise, and after September 11, India's contention about terrorism is beginning to be heard with respect.

India and the Indian culture have made a distinct impact the world over. No super market chain—from Tesco to Sainsbury's—is complete without a line up of Indian food.

Today India has more information workers than Japan and about the same numbers as the United States. So, India has an Information Society within the nation of one billion people. An estimated eighty thousand Indian professionals work for Silicon Valley hightech companies. Nearly 40 per cent of all new start-ups in Silicon Valley have Indian co-founders.

Migrant Indian cyber workers signify the competitive advantage that the Indians hold in the cut throat global information economy, where Indian brain power, computer competence and English langauge skills are key to wealth creation and material success.

India has indeed become a world power in computer software and is an engine of economic growth. The richest people in India—Azim Premji, NR Naryanmurthy, Aditya Birla are all billionaire—owners of IT industries. Whether it is telecommunication, IT or Internet, India is making a rapid headway. Since most Internet communication is in English language, India has huge advantage over other nations. This combination of English language ability and large number of IT professionals in India has boosted country's position world wide in computer software development and in remote processing services. The result is that the Indians now hold senior management positions in US high-tech corporations like Microsoft, Yahoo, Intel and Bell Labs.

Apart from centres of excellence in academics and research, institutions like IITs and IIMs, a number of technopolis, including Hyderabad, NOIDA, Gurgaon and Mohali have become places where the future of India as the emerging power of the 21st century lies.

There is new spring of hope which is so infectious wherever the Indians are :

It is sometimes suggested that there is more of hype than substance in the euphoria built up as a result of IT revolution, just as it was proved that the slogan of India Shining in the 2004 parliamentary elections did not work. There is no doubt that India is beset with several problems of gigantic proportions—uncontrolled population growth, 360 million people leading a poor quality of life, one-third population still illiterate and several others. But, at the same time the country has come out of the vicious circle of stagnant economic growth. It looks towards the future with a sense of achievement, optimism and hope. And that is the real contribution of India to the global information revolution.

NOTE

This chapter draws on the book—*India's Communication Revolution : From Bullock Carts to Cyber Marts* (2001) by Arvind Singhal and Everett M. Rogers, Sage Publication, New Delhi.

REFERENCES

Dicken Peter (1998) *Global Shift : Transforming the World Economy,* Paul Chapman Publishing Ltd., London.

India 2004 (A Reference Annual) Publication Division, Ministry of Information and Broadcasting, Government of India, New Delhi.

India Tomorrow : The Millennium Agenda, Special Millennium Issue, October 2000, Living Media India Ltd., New Delhi.

ANNEXURES

ANNEXURE I

MacBride Commission Report

Conclusions and Recommendations

The survey contained in this Report has recorded a dramatic expansion of communication resources and possibilities. It is an expansion that promises great opportunities, but also raises anxieties and uncertainties. Everything will depend on the use made of the new resources—that is, on crucial decisions, and on the question of who will make the decisions. Communication can be an instrument of power, a revolutionary weapon, a commercial product, or a means of education; it can serve the ends of either liberation or of oppression, of either the growth of the individual personality or of drilling human beings into uniformity. Each society must choose the best way to approach the task facing all of us and to find the means to overcome the material, social and political constraints that impede progress.

We have already considered many suggestions for further development. Without repeating them it might be useful to begin our recommendations by summarizing previous main conclusions:

1. Our review of communication the world over reveals a variety of solutions adopted in different countries—in accordance with diverse traditions, patterns of social, economic and cultural life, needs and possibilities. This diversity is valuable and should be respected; there is no place for the universal application of preconceived models. Yet it should be possible to establish, in broad outline, common aims and common values in the sphere of communication, based on common interests in a world of interdependence. The whole human race is threatened by the arms race and by the persistence of unacceptable global inequalities, both of which generate tensions and which jeopardize its future and even its survival.

The contemporary situation demands a better, more just and more democratic social order, and the realization of fundamental human rights. These goals can be achieved only through understanding and tolerance, gained in large part by free, open and balanced communications.

2. The review has also shown that the utmost importance should be given to eliminating imbalances and disparities in communication and its structures, and particularly in information flows. Developing countries need to reduce their dependence, and claim a new, more just and more equitable order in the field of communication. This issue has been fully debated in various settings; the time has now come to move from principles to substantive reforms and concrete action.

3. Our conclusions are founded on the firm conviction that communication is a basic individual right, as well as a collective one required by all communities and nations. Freedom of information—and, more specifically the right to seek, receive and impart information—is a fundamental human right; indeed, a prerequisite for many others. The inherent nature of communication means that its fullest possible exercise and potential depend on the surrounding political, social and economic conditions, the most vital of these being democracy within countries and equal democratic relations between them. It is in this context that the democratization of communication at national and international levels, as well as the larger role of communication in democratizing society, acquires utmost importance.

4. For these purposes, it is essential to develop comprehensive national communication policies linked to overall social, cultural and economic development objectives. Such policies should evolve from broad consultations with all sectors concerned and adequate mechanisms for wide participation of organized social groups in their definition and implementation. National Governments as much as the international community should recognize the urgency of according communications higher priority in planning and funding. Every country should develop its communication patterns in accordance with its own conditions, needs and traditions, thus strengthening its integrity, independence and self-reliance.

5. The basic considerations which are developed at length in the body of our Report are intended to provide a framework for the development of a new information and communication order. We see its implementation as an on-going process of change in the nature of relations between and within nations in the field of communications. Imbalances in national information and communication systems are as disturbing and unacceptable as social, economic, cultural and technological, both national and international disparities. Indeed, rectification of the latter is inconcievable in any true or lasting sense without elimination of the former. Crucial decisions concerning communication development need to be taken urgently, at both national and international levels. These decisions are not merely the concern of professionals, researchers or scholars, nor can they be the sole prerogative of those holding political or economic power. The decision-making process has to involve social participation at all levels. This calls for new attitudes for overcoming stereotyped thinking and to promote more understanding of diversity and plurality, with full respect for the dignity and equality of peoples living in different conditions and acting in different ways.

Thus our call for reflection and action is addressed broadly to governments and international organizations, to policy-makers and planners, to the media and professional organizations, to researchers, communication practitioners, to organized social groups and the public at large.

Strengthening Independence and Self-reliance

Communication Policies

1. Communication be no longer regarded merely as an incidental service and its development left to chance. Recognition of its potential warrants the formulation by all nations, and particularly developing countries, of comprehensive communication policies linked to overall social, cultural, economic and political goals. Such policies should be based on inter-ministerial and inter-disciplinary consultations with broad public participation. The object must be to utilize

the unique capacities of each form of communication, from interpersonal and traditional to the most modern, to make men and societies aware of their rights, harmonize unity in diversity, and foster the growth of individuals and communities within the wider frame of national development in an interdependent world.

2. As language embodies the cultural experience of people, all languages should be adequately developed to serve the complex and diverse requirements of modern communication. Developing nations and multilingual societies need to evolve language policies that promote all national languages even while selecting some, where necessary, for more widespread use in communication, higher education and administration. There is also need in certain situations for the adaptation, simplification, and standardization of scripts and development of keyboards, preparation of dictionaries and modernized system of language learning, transcription of literature in widely-spoken national languages. The provision of simultaneous interpretation and automated translation facilities now under experimentation for cross-cultural communication to bridge linguistic divides should also be envisaged.

3. A primary policy objective should be to make elementary education available to all and to wipe out illiteracy, supplementing formal schooling systems with non-formal education and enrichment within appropriate structures of continuing and distance learning (through radio, television and correspondence).

4. Within the framework of national development policies, each country will have to work out its own set of priorities, bearing in mind that it will not be possible to move in all directions at the same time. But, as far as resources allow, communication policies should aim at stimulating and encouraging all means of communication.

Strengthening Capacities

5. Developing countries take specific measures to establish or develop essential elements of their communication systems:

print media, broadcasting and telecommunications along with the related training and production facilities.

6. Strong national news agencies are vital for improving each country's national and international reporting. Where viable, regional networks should be set up to increase news flows and serve all the major language groups in the area. Nationally, the agencies should buttress the growth of both urban and rural newspapers to serve as the core of a country's news collection and distribution system.

7. National book production should be encouraged and accompanied by the establishment of a distribution network for books, newspapers and periodicals. The stimulation of works by national authors in various languages should be promoted.

8. The development of comprehensive national radio networks, capable of reaching remote areas should take priority over the development of television, which, however, should be encouraged where appropriate. Special attention should be given to areas where illiteracy is prevalent.

9. National capacity for producing broadcast materials is necessary to obviate dependence on external sources over and beyond desirable programme exchange. This capacity should include national or regional broadcasting, film and documentary production centres with a basic distribution network.

10. Adequate educational and training facilities are required to supply personnel for the media and production organizations, as well as managers, technicians and maintenance personnel. In this regard, co-operation between neighbouring countreis and within region should be encouraged.

Basic Needs

11. The communication component in all development projects should receive adequate financing. So-called "development support communications" are essential for mobilizing initiatives and providing information required for action in all fields of development—agriculture, health and family planning, education, religion, industry and so on.

12. Essential communication needs to be met include the extension of basic postal services and telecommunication networks through small rural electronic exchanges.

13. The development of a community press in rural areas and small towns would not only provide print support for economic and social extension activities. This would also facilitate the production of functional literature for neo-literates as well.

14. Utilization of local radio, low-cost small format television and video systems and other appropriate technologies would facilitate production of programmes relevant to community development efforts, stimulate participation and provide opportunity for diversified cultural expression.

15. The educational and informational use of communication should be given equal priority with entertainment. At the same time, education systems should prepare young people for communication activities. Introduction of pupils at primary and secondary levels to the forms of uses of the means of communication (how to read newspapers, evaluate radio and television programmes, use elementary audio-visual techniques and apparatus) should permit the young to understand reality better and enrich their knowledge of current affairs and problems.

16. Organization of community listening and viewing groups could in certain circumstances widen both entertainment and educational opportunities. Education and information activities should be supported by different facilities ranging from mobile book, tape and film libraries to programmed instruction through "schools of the air".

17. Such activities should be aggregated wherever possible in order to create vibrant local communication resource centres for entertainment, education, information dissemination and cultural exchange. They should be supported by decentralized media production centres; educational and extension services should be location-specific if they are to be credible and accepted.

18. It is not sufficient to urge that communication be given a high priority in national development; possible sources

of investment finance must be identified. Among these could be differential communication pricing policies that would place larger burdens on more prosperous urban and elite groups; the taxing of commercial advertising may also be envisaged for this purpose.

Particular Challenges

19. A major international research and development effort to increase the supply of paper. The worldwide shortage of paper, including newsprint, and its escalating cost impose crushing burdens upon struggling newspapers, periodicals and the publication industry, above all in the developing countries. Certain ecological constraints have also emerged. UNESCO, in collaboration with FAO, should take urgent measures to identify and encourage production of paper and newsprint either by recycling paper or from new sources of feedstock in addition to the wood pulp presently produced largely by certain northern countries. Kenaf, bagasse, tropical woods and grasses could possibly provide alternative sources. Initial experiments are encouraging and need to be supported and multiplied.

20. Tariffs for news transmission, telecommunications rates and air mail charges for the dissemination of news, transport of newspapers, periodicals, books and audiovisual materials are one of the main obstacles to a free and balanced flow of information. This situation must be corrected, especially in the case of developing countries, through a variety of national and international initiaives. Governments should in particular examime the policies and practices of their post and telegraph authorities. Profits or revenues should not be the primary aim of such agencies. They are instruments for policy-making and planned development in the field of information and culture. Their tariffs should be in line with larger national goals. International action is also necessary to alter telecommunication tariffs that militate heavily against small and peripheral users. Current international consultations of this question may be brought to early fruition, possibly at the

October 1980 session of the 154-nation International Telegraph and Telephone Consultative Committee, which should have before it specific proposals made by a UNESCO-sponsored working group on "Low Telecommunication Rates" (November 1979). UNESCO might, in cooperation with ITU, also sponsor an overall study on international telecommunication services by means of satellite transmission in collaboration with Intelsat, Intersputnik and user country representatives to make proposals for international and regional coordination of geostationary satellite development. The study should also include investigation of the possibility and practicalities of discounts for transmission of news and preferential rates for certain types of transmission to and from developing countries. Finally, developing countries should investigate the possibility of negotiating preferential tariffs on a bilateral or regional basis.

21. The electro-magnetic spectrum and geostationary orbit, both finite natural resources, should be more equitably shared as the common property of mankind. For that purpose, we welcome the decisions taken by the World Administrative Radio Conference (WARC), Geneva, September–November 1979, to convene a series of special conferences over the next few years on certain specific topics related to the utilization of these resources.

Social Consequences and New Tasks

Integrating Communication into Development

22. Promotion of dialogue for development as a central component of both communication and development policies. Implementation of national policies should be carried out through three complementary communication patterns: first, from decision-makers towards different social sectors to transmit information about what they regard as necessary changes in development actions, alternative strategies and the varying consequences of the different alternatives; second, among and between diverse social sectors in a horizontal

information network to express and exchange views on their different demands, aspirations, objective needs and subjective motivations; third, between decision-makers and all social groups through permanent participatory mechanisms for two-way information flows to elaborate development goals and priorities and make decisions on utilization of resources. Each one of these patterns requires the design of specific information programmes, using different communication means.

23. In promoting communication policies, special attention should be given to the use of non-technical language and comprehensible symbols, images and forms to ensure popular understanding of development issues and goals. Similarly, development information supplied to the media should be adapted to prevailing news values and practices, which is turn should be encouraged to be more receptive to development needs and problems.

Facing the Technological Challenge

24. Devising policy instruments at the national level in order to evaluate the positive and negative social implications of the introduction of powerful new communication technologies. The preparation of technological impact surveys can be a useful tool to assess the consequences for life styles, relevance for under-privileged sectors of society, cultural influence, effects on employment patterns, and similar factors. This is particularly important when making choices with respect to the development of communication infrastructures.

25. Setting up national mechanisms to promote participation and discussion of social priorities in the acquisition or extension of new communication technologies. Decisions with respect to the orientation given to research and development should come under closer public scrutiny.

26. In developing countries the promotion of autonomous research and development should be linked to specific projects and programmes at the national, regional and inter-regional levels, which are often geared to the satisfaction of basic needs. More funds are necessary to stimulate and support adaptive

technological research. This might also help these countries to avoid problems of obsolescence and problems arising from the non-availability of particular types of equipment, related spare parts and components from the advanced industrial nations.

27. The concentration of communications technology in a relatively few developed countries and transnational corporations has led to virtual monopoly situations in this field. To counteract these tendencies national and international measures are required, among them reform of existing patent laws and conventions, appropriate legislation and international agreements.

Strengthening Cultural Identity

28. Establishment of national cultural policies, which should foster cultural identity and creativity, and involve the media in these tasks. Such policies should also contain guidelines for safeguarding national cultural development while promoting knowledge of other cultures. It is in relation to others that each culture enhances its own identity.

29. Communication and cultural policies should ensure that creative artists and various grass-root groups can make their voices heard through the media. The innovative uses of film, television or radio by people of different cultures should be studied. Such experiments constitute a basis for continuing cultural dialogue, which could be furthered by agreements between countries and through international support.

30. Introduction of guidelines with respect to advertising content and the values and attitudes it fosters, in accordance with national standards and practices. Such guidelines should be consistent with national development policies and efforts to preserve cultural identity. Particular attention should be given to the impact on children and adolescents. In this connection, various mechanisms such as complaint boards or consumer review committees might be established to afford the public the possibility of reacting against advertising which they feel inappropriate.

Reducing the Commercialization of Communication

31. In expanding communication systems, preference should be given to non-commercial forms of mass communication. Promotion of such types of communication should be integrated with the traditions, culture, development objectives and socio-political system of each country. As in the field of education, public funds might be made available for this purpose.

32. While acknowledging the need of the media for revenues, ways and means should be considered to reduce the negative effects that the influence of market and commercial considerations have in the organization and content of national and international communication flows.

33. That consideration be given to changing existing funding patterns of commercial mass media. In this connection, reviews could be made of the way in which the relative role of advertising volume and costs pricing policies, voluntary contributions, subsidies, taxes, financial incentives and supports could be modified to enhance the social function of mass media and improve their service to the community.

34. Developing countries should pay particular attention to: (a) the correlation between education, scientific and communication policies, because their practical application frequently overlaps; (b) the creation in each country of one or several centres for the collection and utilization of technical information and data, both from within the country and from abroad; (c) to secure the basic equipment necessary for essential data processing activities; (d) the development of skills and facilities for computer processing and analysis of data obtained from remote sensing.

35. Developed countries should foster exchanges of technical information on the principle that all countries have equal rights to full access to available information. It is increasingly necessary, in order to reduce inequalities in this field, to promote cooperative arrangements for collection, retrieval, processing and diffusion of technological information through various networks, regardless of geographical or institutional frontiers. UNISIST, which provides basic

guidelines for voluntary cooperation among and between information systems and services, should further develop its activities.

36. Developing countries should adopt national informatics policies as a matter of priority. These should primarily relate to the establishment of decision-making centres (inter-departmental and inter-disciplinary) which would inter alia (a) assess technological alternatives; (b) centralize purchases; (c) encourage local production of software; (d) promote regional and sub-regional cooperation (in various fields, including education, health and consumer services).

37. At the international level, consideration should be given to action with respect to: (a) a systematic identification of existing organized data processing infrastructures in various specialized fields; (b) agreement on measures for effective multi-country participation in the programmes, planning and administration of existing or developing data infrastructures; (c) analysis of commercial and technical measures likely to improve the use of informatics by developing countries; (d) agreement on international priorities for research and development that is of interest to all countries in the field of informatics.

38. Transnational corporations should supply to the authorities of the countries in which they operate, upon request and on a regular basis as specified by local laws and regulations, all information required for legislative and administrative purposes relevant to their activities and specifically needed to assess the performance of such entities. They should also provide the public, trade unions and other interested sectors of the countries in which they operate with information needed to understand the global structure, activities and policies of the transnational corporations and their significance for the country concerned.

Professional Integrity and Standards

39. The importance of the journalist's mission in the contemporary world demands steps to enhance his standing in

society. In many countries even today, journalists are not regarded as members of an acknowledged profession and they are treated accordingly. To overcome this situation, journalism needs to raise its standards and quality for recognition everywhere as a genuine profession.

40. To be treated as professionals, journalists require broad educational preparation and specific professional training. Programmes of instruction need to be developed not only for entry-level recruits, but also for experienced personnel who from time to time would behefit from special seminars and conferences designed to refresh and enrich their qualifications. Basically, programmes of instruction and training should be conducted on national and regional levels.

41. Such values as truthfulness, accuracy and *respect for human rights* are not universally applied at present. Higher professional standards and responsibility cannot be imposed by decree, nor do they depend solely on the goodwill of individual journalists, who are employed by institutions which can improve or handicap their professional performance. The self-respect of journalists, their integrity and inner drive to turn out work of high quality are of paramount importance. It is this level of professional dedication, making for responsibility, that should be fostered by news media and journalists' organizations. In this framework, a distinction may have to be drawn between media institutions, owners and managers on the one hand, and journalists on the other.

42. As in other professions, journalists and media organizations serve the public directly and the public, in turn, is entitled to hold them accountable for their actions. Among the mechanisms devised upto now in various countries for assuring accountability, the Commission sees merit in press or media councils, the institution of the press ombudsman and peer group criticism of the sort practised by journalism reviews in several countries. In addition, communities served by particular media can accomplish significant reforms through citizen action. Specific forms of community involvement in decision-making will vary, of course, from country to country. Public broadcasting stations, for example, can be governed by

representative boards drawn from the community. Voluntary measures of this sort can do much to influence media performance. Nevertheless, it appears necessary to develop further effective ways by which the right to assess mass media performance can be exercised by the public.

43. Codes of professional ethics exist in all parts of the world, adopted voluntarily in many countries by professional groups. The adoption of codes of ethics at national and, in some cases, at the regional level is desirable, provided that such codes are prepared and adopted by the profession itself—without governmental interference.

Towards Improved International Reporting

44. All countries should take steps to assure admittance of foreign correspondents and facilitate their collection and transmission of news. Special obligations in this regard, undertaken by the signatories to the Final Act of the Helsinki conference, should be honoured and, indeed, liberally applied. Free access to news sources by journalists is an indispensable requirement for accurate, faithful and balanced reporting. This necesarily involves access to unofficial, as well as official sources of information, that is, access to the entire spectrum of opinion within any country.

45. Conventional standards of news selection and reporting, and many accepted news values, need to be reassessed if readers and listeners around the world are to receive a more faithful and comprehensive account of events, movements and trends in both developing and developed countries. The inescapable need to interpret unfamiliar situations in terms that will be understood by a distant audience should not blind reporters or editors to the hazards of narrow ethnocentric thinking. The first step towards overcoming this bias is to acknowledge that it colours the thinking of virutally all human beings, journalists included, for the most part without deliberate intent. The act of selecting certain news items for publication, while rejecting others, produces in the minds of the audience a picture of the world that may well be incomplete or distorted. Higher professional standards are needed for

journalists to be able to illuminate the diverse cultures and beliefs of the modern world, without their presuming to judge the ultimate validity of any foreign nation's experience and traditions.

46. To this end, reporters being assigned to foreign posts should have the benefit of langauge training and acquaintance with the history, institutions, politics, economics and cultural environment of the country or region in which they will be serving.

47. The press and broadcasters in the industrialized world should allot more space and time to reporting events in and background material about foreign countries in general and news from the developing world in particular. Also, the media in developed countries—especially the "gatekeepers", editors and producers of print and broadcasting media who select the news items to be published or broadcast—should become more familiar with the cultures and conditions in developing countries. Although the present imbalance in news flows calls for strengthening capacities in developing countries, the media of the industrialized countries have their contribution to make towards the correction of these inequalities.

48. To offset the negative effects of inaccurate or malicious reporting of international news, the right of reply and correction should be further considered. While these concepts are recognized in many countries, their nature and scope vary so widely that it would be neither expedient nor realistic to propose the adoption of any international regulations for their purpose. False or distorted news accounts can be harmful, but the voluntary publication of corrections or replies is preferable to international normative action. Since the manner in which the right of reply and correction as applied in different countries varies significantly, it is further suggested that: (a) the exercise of the international right of reply and correction be considered for application on a voluntary basis in each country according to its journalistic practices and national legal framework; (b) the United Nations, in consultation with all concerned bodies, explore the conditions under which this right could be perfected at the international level, taking into account the

cumbersome operation of the 1952 Convention on the International Right of Correction; (c) media institutions with an international reach define on a voluntary basis internal standards for the exercise of this right and make them publicly available.

49. Intelligence services of many nations have at one time or other recruited journalists to commit espionage under cover of their professional duties. This practice must be condemned. It undermines the integrity of the profession and, in some circumstances, can expose other journalists to unjustified suspicion or physical threat. The Commission urges journalists and their employers to be on guard against possible attempts of this kind. We also urge governments to refrain from using journalists for purposes of espionage.

Protection of Journalists

50. The professional independence and integrity of all those involved in the collection and dissemination of news, information and views to the public should be safeguarded. However, the Commission does not propose special privileges to protect journalists in the performance of their duties, although journalism is often a dangerous profession. Far from constituting a special category, journalists are citizens of their respective countries, entitled to the same range of human rights as other citizens. One exception is provided in the Additional Protocol to the Geneva Conventions of 12 August 1949, which applies only to journalists on perilous missions, such as in areas of armed conflict. To propose additional measures would invite the dangers entailed in a licensing system since it would require some body to stipulate who should be entitled to claim such protection. Journalists will be fully protected only when everyone's human rights are guaranteed.

51. That UNESCO should convene a series of round tables at which journalists, media executives, researchers and jurists can periodically review problems related to the protection of journalists and propose additional appropriate measures to this end.

Democratization of Communication

52. All those working in the mass media should contribute to the fulfilment of human rights, both individual and collective, in the spirit of the UNESCO Declaration on the mass media and the International Bill of Human Rights. The contribution of the media in this regard is not only to foster these principles, but also to expose all infringements, wherever they occur, and to support those whose rights have been neglected or violated. Professional associations and public opinion should support journalists subject to pressure or who suffer adverse consequences from their dedication to the defence of human rights.

53. The media should contribute to promoting the just cause of peoples struggling for freedom and independence and their right to live in peace and equality without foreign interference. This is especially important for all oppressed peoples who, while struggling against religious and racial discrimination, are deprived of opportunity to make their voices heard within their own countries.

54. Communication needs in a democratic society should be met by the extension of specific rights such as the right to be informed, the right to inform, the right to privacy, the right to participate in public communication—all elements of a new concept, the right to communicate. In developing what might be called a new era of social rights, we suggest all the implications of the right to communicate be further explored.

Removal of Obstacles

55. All countries adopt measures to enlarge sources of information needed by citizens in their everyday life. A careful review of existing laws and regulations should be undertaken with the aim of reducing limitations, secrecy provisions and other constraints in information practices.

56. Censorship or arbitrary control of information should be abolished. In areas where reasonable restrictions may be

considered necessary, these should be provided for by law, subject to judicial review and in line with the principles enshrined in the United Nations Charter, the Universal Declaration of Human Rights and the International Covenants relating to human rights, and in other instruments adopted by the community of nations.

57. Special attention should be devoted to obstacles and restrictions which derive from the concentration of media ownership, public or private, from commercial influences on the press and broadcasting, or from private or governmental advertising. The problem of financial conditions under which the media operate should be critically reviewed, and measures elaborated to strengthen editorial independence.

58. Effective legal measures should be designed to: (a) limit the process of concentration and monopolization; (b) circumscribe the action of transnationals by requiring them to comply with specific criteria and conditions defined by national legislation and development policies; (c) reverse trends to reduce the number of decision-makers at a time when the media's public is growing larger and the impact of communication is increasing; (d) reduce the influence of advertising upon editorial policy and broadcast programming; (e) seek and improve models which would ensure greater independence and autonomy of the media concerning their management and editorial policy, whether these media are under private, public or government ownership.

Diversity and Choice

59. The building of infrastructures and the adoption of particular technologies should be carefully matched to the need for more abundant information to a broader public from a plurality of sources.

60. Attention should be paid to the communication needs of women. They should be assured adequate access to communication means and that images of them and of their activities are not distorted by the media or in advertising.

61. The concerns of children and youth, national, ethnic, religious, linguistic minorities, people living in remote areas and the aged and handicapped also deserve particular consideration. They constitute large and sensitive segments of society and have special communication needs.

62. Much more attention be devoted to use of the media in living and working environments. Instead of isolating men and women, the media should help integrate them into the community.

63. Readers, listeners and viewers have generally been treated as passive receivers of information. Those in-charge of the media should encourage their audiences to play a more active role in communication by allocating more newspaper space, or braodcasting time, for the views of individual members of the public or organized social groups.

64. The creation of appropriate communication facilities at all levels, leading towards new forms of public involvement in the management of the media and new modalities for their funding.

65. Communication policy makers should give far grater importance to devising ways whereby the management of the media could be democratized—while respecting national customs and characteristics—by associating the following categories: (a) journalists and professional communicators; (b) creative artists; (c) technicians; (d) media owners and managers; (e) representatives of the public. Such democratization of the media needs the full support and understanding of all those working in them, and this process should lead to their having a more active role in editorial policy and management.

Fostering International Cooperation

Partners for Development

66. The progressive implementation of national and international measures that will foster the setting up of a new

world information and communication order. The proposals contained in this report can serve as a contribution to develop the varied actions necessary to move in that direction.

67. International cooperation for the development of communications be given equal priority with and within other sectors (e.g. health, agriculture, industry, science, education, etc.) as infromation is a basic resource for individual and collective advancement and for all-round development. This may be achieved by utilizing funds provided through bilateral govermental agreements and from international and regional organizations, which should plan a considerable increase in their allocations for communication, infrastructures, equipment and programme development. Care should be taken that the assistance is compatible with developing countries' priorities. Consideration should also be given to provision of assistance on a programme rather than on a strict project basis.

68. The close relationship between the establishment of a new international economic order and the new world information and communication order should be carefully considered by the technical bodies dealing with these issues. Concrete plans of action linking both processes should be implemented within the United Nations system. The United Nations, in approving the international development strategy should consider the communications sector as an integral element of it and not merely as an instrument of public information.

Strengthening Collective Self-reliance

69. The communication dimension should be incorporated into existing programmes and agreements for economic cooperation between developing countries.

70. Joint activities in the field of communication, which are under way between developing countries should be developed further in the light of the overall analysis and recommendations of this Report. In particular, attention should be given to cooperation among national news agencies, to the

further development of the News Agencies Pool and broadcasting organizations of the non-aligned countries, as well as to the general exchange on a regular basis of radio, TV programmes and films.

71. With respect to cooperation in the field of technical information, the establishment of regional and sub-regional data banks and information processing centres and specialized documentation centres should be given a high priority. They should be conceived and organized, both in terms of software and management, according to the particular needs of cooperating countries. Choices of technology and selection of foreign enterprises should be made so as not to increase dependence in this field.

72. Mechanisms for sharing information of a non-strategic nature could be established particularly in economic matters. Arrangements of this nature could be of value in areas such as multilateral trade negotiations, dealings with transnational corporations and banks, economic forecasting, and medium- and long-term planning and other similar fields.

73. Particular efforts should be undertaken to ensure that news about other developing countries within or outside their region receive more attention and space in the media. Special projects could be developed to ensure a steady flow of attractive and interesting material inspired by news values which meet developing countries' infromation needs.

74. Measures to promote links and agreements between professional organizations and communication researchers of different countries should be fostered. It is necessary to develop networks of institutions and people working in the field of communicatin in order to share and exhange experiences and implement joint projects of common interest with concrete operational contents.

International Mechanisms

75. The Member States of UNESCO should increase their support to the Organization's programme in this area. Consideration

should be given to organizing a distinct communication sector, not simply in order to underline its importance, but to emphasize that its activities are inter-related with the other major components of UNESCO's work—education, science and culture. In its communications activities, UNESCO should concentrate on priority areas. Among these are assistance to national policy formulation and planning, technical development, organizing professional meetings and exchanges, promotion and coordination of research, and elaboration of international norms.

76. Better coordination of the various communication activities within UNESCO and those throughout the United Nations System. A thorough inventory and assessment of all communication development related programmes of the various agencies should be undertaken as a basis for designing appropriate mechanisms to carry out the necessary consultation, cooperation and coordination.

77. It would be desirable for the United Nations family to be equipped with a more effective information system, including a broadcast capability of its own and possibly access to a satellite system. That would enable the United Nations to follow more closely world affairs and transmit its message more effectively to all the peoples of the earth. Although such a proposal would require heavy investment and raise some complex issues, a feasibility study should be undertaken so that a carefully designed project could be prepared for deliberation and decision.

78. Consideration might be given to establishing within the framework of UNESCO an International Centre for the Study and Planning of Information and Communication. Its main tasks would be to: (a) promote the development of national communication systems in developing countries and the balance and reciprocity in international information flows; (b) mobilize resources required for that purpose and manage the funds put at its disposal; and (c) assure coordination among parties interested in communication development and involved in various cooperation programmes and evaluate

results of bilateral and multilateral activities in this field; (d) organize round tables, seminars, and conferences for the training of communication planners, researchers and journalists, particularly those specializing in international problems; and (e) keep under review communications technology transfers between developed and developing countries so that they are carried out in the most suitable conditions. The Centre may be guided by a tripartite coordinating council composed of representatives of developing and developed countries and of interested international organizations. We suggest UNESCO should undertake further study of this proposal for consideration at the 1980 session of the General Conference.

Towards International Understanding

The strengthening of peace, international security and cooperation and the lessening of international tensions are the common concern of all nations. The mass media can make a substantial contribution towards achieving these goals. The speical session of the United Nations General Assembly on disarmament called for increased efforts by the mass media to mobilize public opinion in favour of disarmament and of ending the arms race. This Declaration together with the UNESCO Declaration on fundamental principles concerning the contribution of the mass media to strengthening peace and international understanding, to the promotion of human rights and to countering racialism, apartheid and incitement to war should be the foundation of new communication policies to foster international understanding. A new world information and communication order requires and must become the instrument for peaceful cooperation between nations.

79. National communication policies should be consistent with adopted international communication principles and should seek to create a climate of mutual understanding and peaceful coexistence among nations. Countries should also encourage their broadcast and other means of international communication to make the fullest contribution towards peace

and international cooperation and to refrain from advocating national, racial or religious hatred, and incitement to discrimination, hostility, violence or war.

80. Due attention should be paid to the problems of peace and disarmament, human rights, development and the creation of a new communication order. Mass media both printed and audiovisual, should be encouraged to publicise significant documents of the United Nations, of UNESCO, of the world peace movements, and of various other international and national organizations devoted to peace and disarmament. The curricula of schools of journalism should include study of these international problems and the views expressed on them within the United Nations.

81. All forms of co-operation among the media, the professionals and their associations, which contribute to the better knowledge of other nations and cultures, should be encouraged and promoted.

82. Reporting on international events or developments in individual countries in situations of crisis and tension requires extreme care and responsibility. In such situations the media often constitute one of the few, if not the sole, link between combatants or hostile groups. This clearly casts on them a special role which they should seek to discharge with objectivity and sensitivity.

❑ ❑ ❑

The recommendations and suggestions contained in our Report do not presume to cover all topics and issues calling for reflection and action. Nevertheless, they indicate the importance and scale of the tasks which face every country in the field of information and communication, as well as their international dimensions which pose a formidable challenge to the community of nations.

Our study indicates clearly the direction in which the world must move to attain a new information and communication order—essentially a series of new relationship arising from the advances promised by new communication technologies which should enable all peoples to benefit. The awareness already created on certain issues, such as global imbalances in information flows, suggests that a process of change has resulted and is under way. The power and promise of ever-new communication technologies and systems are, however, such as to demand deliberate measures to ensure that existing communication disparities do not widen. The objective should be to ensure that men and women are enabled to lead richer and more satisfying lives.

NOTE

This Annexure has been adapted from the Report of the International Commission for the Study of Communication Problems established by the UNESCO in 1977. The Commission is also known as MacBride Commission, so termed after the name of its Chairman Sean MacBride. The Report has been titled as; *Many Voices, One World : Communication and Society,* Today and Tomorrow.

ANNEXURE II

all human rights for all

FIFTIETH ANNIVERSARY OF THE UNIVERSAL DECLARATION OF HUMAN RIGHTS

1948-1998

UNIVERSAL DELARATION OF HUMAN RIGHTS

Adopted and proclaimed by General Assembly resolution 217 A (III) of 10 December 1948

On December 10, 1948 the General Assembly of the United Nations adopted and proclaimed the Universal Declaration of Human Rights the full text of which appears in the following pages. Following this historic act the Assembly called upon all Member countries to publicize the text of the Declaration and "to cause it to be disseminated, displayed, read and expounded principally in schools and other educational institutions, without distinction based on the political status of countries or territories."

Preamble

Whereas recognition of the inherent dignity and of the equal and inalienable rights of all members of the human family is the foundation of freedom, justice and peace in the world,

Whereas disregard and contempt for human rights have resulted in barbarous acts which have outraged the conscience of mankind, and the advent of a world in which human beings shall enjoy freedom of speech and belief and freedom from fear and want has been proclaimed as the highest aspiration of the common people,

Whereas it is essential, if man is not to be compelled to have recourse, as a last resort, to rebellion against tyranny and oppression, that human rights should be protected by the rule of law,

Whereas it is essential to promote the development of friendly relations between nations,

Whereas the peoples of the United Nations have in the Charter reaffirmed their faith in fundamental human rights, in the dignity and worth of the human person and in the equal rights of men and women and have determined to promote social progress and better standards of life in larger freedom,

Whereas Member States have pledged themselves to achieve, in co-operation with the United Nations, the promotion of universal respect for and observance of human rights and fundamental freedoms,

Whereas a common understanding of these rights and freedoms is of the greatest importance for the full realization of this pledge,

Now, Therefore the General Assembly proclaims this Universal Declaration of Human Rights as a common standard of achievement for all peoples and all nations, to the end that every individual and every organ of society, keeping this Declaration constantly in mind, shall strive by teaching and education to promote respect for these rights and freedoms and by progressive measures, national and international, to secure their universal and effective recognition and observance, both among the peoples of Member States themselves and among the peoples of territories under their jurisdiction.

Article 1.

All human beings are born free and equal in dignity and rights.They are endowed with reason and conscience and should act towards one another in a spirit of brotherhood.

Article 2.

Everyone is entitled to all the rights and freedoms set forth in this Declaration, without distinction of any kind, such as race, colour, sex, language, religion, political or other opinion, national or social origin, property, birth or other status. Furthermore, no distinction shall be made on the basis of the political, jurisdictional or international status of the country or territory to which a person belongs, whether it be independent, trust, non-self-governing or under any other limitation of sovereignty.

Article 3.

Everyone has the right to life, liberty and security of person.

Article 4.

No one shall be held in slavery or servitude; slavery and the slave trade shall be prohibited in all their forms.

Article 5.

No one shall be subjected to torture or to cruel, inhuman or degrading treatment or punishment.

Article 6.

Everyone has the right to recognition everywhere as a person before the law.

Article 7.

All are equal before the law and are entitled without any discrimination to equal protection of the law. All are entitled to equal protection against any discrimination in violation of this Declaration and against any incitement to such discrimination.

Article 8.

Everyone has the right to an effective remedy by the competent national tribunals for acts violating the fundamental rights granted him by the constitution or by law.

Article 9.

No one shall be subjected to arbitrary arrest, detention or exile.

Article 10.

Everyone is entitled in full equality to a fair and public hearing by an independent and impartial tribunal, in the determination of his rights and obligations and of any criminal charge against him.

Article 11.

(1) Everyone charged with a penal offence has the right to be presumed innocent until proved guilty according to law in a public trial at which he has had all the guarantees necessary for his defence.

(2) No one shall be held guilty of any penal offence on account of any act or omission which did not constitute a penal offence, under national or international law, at the time when it was committed. Nor shall a heavier penalty be imposed than the one that was applicable at the time the penal offence was committed.

Article 12.

No one shall be subjected to arbitrary interference with his privacy, family, home or correspondence, nor to attacks upon his honour and reputation. Everyone has the right to the protection of the law against such interference or attacks.

Article 13.

(1) Everyone has the right to freedom of movement and residence within the borders of each state.

(2) Everyone has the right to leave any country, including his own, and to return to his country.

Article 14.

(1) Everyone has the right to seek and to enjoy in other countries asylum from persecution.

(2) This right may not be invoked in the case of prosecutions genuinely arising from non-political crimes or from acts contrary to the purposes and principles of the United Nations.

Article 15.

(1) Everyone has the right to a nationality.

(2) No one shall be arbitrarily deprived of his nationality nor denied the right to change his nationality.

Article 16.

(1) Men and women of full age, without any limitation due to race, nationality or religion, have the right to marry and to found a family. They are entitled to equal rights as to marriage, during marriage and at its dissolution.

(2) Marriage shall be entered into only with the free and full consent of the intending spouses.

(3) The family is the natural and fundamental group unit of society and is entitled to protection by society and the State.

Article 17.

(1) Everyone has the right to own property alone as well as in association with others.

(2) No one shall be arbitrarily deprived of his property.

Article 18.

Everyone has the right to freedom of thought, conscience and religion; this right includes freedom to change his religion or belief, and freedom, either alone or in community with others and in public or private, to manifest his religion or belief in teaching, practice, worship and observance.

Article 19.

Everyone has the right to freedom of opinion and expression; this right includes freedom to hold opinions without interference and to seek, receive and impart information and ideas through any media and regardless of frontiers.

Article 20.

(1) Everyone has the right to freedom of peaceful assembly and association.

(2) No one may be compelled to belong to an association.

Article 21.

(1) Everyone has the right to take part in the government of his country, directly or through freely chosen representatives.

(2) Everyone has the right of equal access to public service in his country.

(3) The will of the people shall be the basis of the authority of government; this will shall be expressed in periodic and genuine elections which shall be by universal and equal suffrage and shall be held by secret vote or by equivalent free voting procedures.

Article 22.

Everyone, as a member of society, has the right to social security and is entitled to realization, through national effort and international co-operation and in accordance with the organization and resources of each State, of the economic, social and cultural rights indispensable for his dignity and the free development of his personality.

Article 23.

(1) Everyone has the right to work, to free choice of employment, to just and favourable conditions of work and to protection against unemployment.

(2) Everyone, without any discrimination, has the right to equal pay for equal work.

(3) Everyone who works has the right to just and favourable remuneration ensuring for himself and his family

an existence worthy of human dignity, and supplemented, if necessary, by other means of social protection.

(4) Everyone has the right to form and to join trade unions for the protection of his interests.

Article 24.

Everyone has the right to rest and leisure, including reasonable limitation of working hours and periodic holidays with pay.

Article 25.

(1) Everyone has the right to a standard of living adequate for the health and well-being of himself and of his family, including food, clothing, housing and medical care and necessary social services, and the right to security in the event of unemployment, sickness, disability, widowhood, old age or other lack of livelihood in circumstances beyond his control.

(2) Motherhood and childhood are entitled to special care and assistance. All children, whether born in or out of wedlock, shall enjoy the same social protection.

Article 26.

(1) Everyone has the right to education. Education shall be free, at least in the elementary and fundamental stages. Elementary education shall be compulsory. Technical and professional education shall be made generally available and higher education shall be equally accessible to all on the basis of merit.

(2) Education shall be directed to the full development of the human personality and to the strengthening of respect for human rights and fundamental freedoms. It shall promote understanding, tolerance and friendship among all nations, racial or religious groups, and shall further the activities of the United Nations for the maintenance of peace.

(3) Parents have a prior right to choose the kind of education that shall be given to their children.

Article 27.

(1) Everyone has the right freely to participate in the cultural life of the community, to enjoy the arts and to share in scientific advancement and its benefits.

(2) Everyone has the right to the protection of the moral and material interests resulting from any scientific, literary or artistic production of which he is the author.

Article 28.

Everyone is entitled to a social and international order in which the rights and freedoms set forth in this Declaration can be fully realized.

Article 29.

(1) Everyone has duties to the community in which alone the free and full development of his personality is possible.

(2) In the exercise of his rights and freedoms, everyone shall be subject only to such limitations as are determined by law solely for the purpose of securing due recognition and respect for the rights and freedoms of others and of meeting the just requirements of morality, public order and the general welfare in a democratic society.

(3) These rights and freedoms may in no case be exercised contrary to the purposes and principles of the United Nations.

Article 30.

Nothing in this Declaration may be interpreted as implying for any State, group or person any right to engage in any activity or to perform any act aimed at the destruction of any of the rights and freedoms set forth herein.

Source : www.un.org

ANNEXURE III

STATEMENT ON COMMUNICATION RIGTHS

The statement, presented by Professor Cees Hamelink at the World Forum on Communication Rights, on 11 December 2003, in Geneva, aims at gathering under the name "Communication Rights" a number of existing Human Rights related to information and communication. This statement is there to remind us that the majority of these rights are often ignored on the ground everywhere.

The statement calls for a real practical application of these rights at all the levels.

Vision and Context

Communication plays a central role in politics, economics, and culture in societies across the globe. Information and communication technologies, together with the political will to implement communication rights, can provide vital new opportunities for political interaction, social and economic development, and cultural sustainability. The means to achieve these ends include universal access of all to the means of communication and information and to a diversity of media throughout the world.

Communication is a fundamental social process and the foundation of all social organizations. It is more than the mere transmission of messages. Communication is human interaction among individuals and groups through which identities and meanings are shaped. Communication rights are based on a vision of the free flow of information and ideas which is interactive, egalitarian and non-discriminatory and driven by human needs, rather than commercial or political interests. These rights represent people's claim to freedom, inclusiveness, diversity and participation in the communication process.

Our vision of communication rights is based upon the recognition of the inherent dignity and the equal and inalienable rights of all people.

While recognizing the great potential of communication in contemporary societies, we also draw attention to some of the problems facing full recognition of communication rights. The problem of political control and interference with freedom of expression remains a central concern. Along with media saturation comes a dependency upon the media for knowledge about the world, a dependency that is greater in times of armed conflict. At the same time, the influence of propaganda and censorship has never been so widespread.

Communication has become big global business. Many of its products and services are shaped by commercial goals instead of considerations based on the common good. The global media market is largely controlled by a small number of giant conglomerates, endangering the diversity and independence of information flows. This threat to diversity is heightened by current trends in international trade negotiations, which risk subjecting 'culture' to the same rules as commodities and undermining indigenous culture, knowledge and heritage. On the other hand, strict intellectual property regimes create information enclosures and pose critical obstacles to emerging 'knowledge' societies.

The exclusion of large numbers of people from the democratic political process due to the lack of effective means of participation is another challenge for communication rights. This problem is exacerbated by the expansion of 'around the clock' powers to monitor and intercept communications, justified in the name of security but almost universally abused.

New technologies and a more profound understanding of communication rights have the power to make information and knowledge more readily available to people everywhere and to transform social and political processes. However, much remains to be done for this to become a reality. Global communication remains far from universal, with most of the world's people still excluded from meaningful access to communication, information and the media.

Communication Rights

With the adoption of the Universal Declaration of Human Rights, the international community recognised the inherent dignity of all members of the human family by providing everyone with equal and inalienable rights. Communication rights are intrinsically bound up with the human condition and are based on a new, more powerful understanding of the implications of human rights and the role of communications. Without communication rights, human beings cannot live in freedom, justice, peace and dignity. The recognition of this universal human need has inspired us to set out a statement on communication rights based upon the key principles of *Freedom, Inclusiveness, Diversity and Participation.**

Freedom

The core of communication rights is Article 19 of the Universal Declaration of Human Rights, which proclaims: "Everyone has the right to freedom of expression and opinion; this right includes the freedom to hold opinions without interference and to seek, receive and impart information and ideas through any media and regardless of frontiers." This basic freedom is also recognized in the International Covenant on Civil and Political Rights (Article 19), in other UN treaties, such as the Convention on the Rights of the Child (Article 13), and in all three main regional human rights instruments (Africa, the Americas and Europe).

Despite these guarantees, censorship remains a reality as humankind embarks on the 21st century. Political and commercial pressures on independent news reporting are ever-present and freedom of speech on the Internet is under serious threat in many parts of the world. The right to freedom of expression is also increasingly under threat from significantly enhanced State powers to monitor and intercept communications around the world. It is crucial that the international community adopts robust rules and mechanisms to secure effectively the confidentiality of private communications. It is therefore urgent that we renew global commitment to freedom of information and expression as "the touchstone of all freedoms to which the United Nations is consecrated", as stated in The United Nations General Assembly in Resolution 59(I), adopted at its very first session in 1946.

Inclusiveness

International human rights treaties include many provisions designed to guarantee inclusiveness, such as universal access to information and knowledge, universal access to education, protection of the cultural life of communities and equal sharing of advancements in science and technology. In the current global reality, however, large numbers of people are excluded from access to the basic means of communication, such as telephony, broadcasting and the Internet. Access to information about matters of public concern is also unduly limited, and is also very unequal between and within societies. True commitment to inclusiveness requires the allocation of considerable material and non-material resources by the international community and national governments to overcome these obstacles.

Diversity

Worldwide, existing forms of cultural, informational and linguistic diversity are seriously threatened. Diversity in culture, language and communication is as critical to the sustainability of the planet as the world's biological and natural diversity. Communication diversity is crucial to democracy and political participation, to the right of all people to promote, protect and preserve their cultural identity and the free pursuit of their cultural development.

Diversity is needed at a number of levels including the availability of a wide range of different sources of information, diversity of ownership in the media and forms of access to the media that ensure that the views of all sectors and groups in society are heard.

Participation

International human rights stress the importance of people's participation in political processes which from the perspective of communication rights implies the right to have one's views taken into account. In this context, the equal participation of women and the participation of minorities and marginalized groups is particularly important. Communication is essential to the processes of political decision-making. As the role of media in modern politics expands, this should not obstruct but rather support the participation of people in the political process through the development of participatory governance at all levels

Vision and Reality

Communication rights remain for most of the world's people a vision and an aspiration. They are not a reality on the ground. On the contrary, they are frequently and systematically violated. Governments must be constantly reminded that they are legally required under the human rights treaties they have ratified to implement, promote and protect communication rights. Communication rights are the expression of fundamental needs. The satisfaction of these needs requires a strong political will and the allocation of substantial resources. Lack of commitment to such resources serves only to deepen the global distrust of political institutions.

At the same time, full implementation of communication rights cannot depend only upon governments. Civil society has a key role to play in terms of advocacy for rights, in terms of monitoring and exposing rights abuse and in terms of educating and popularising rights.

Encouraging and facilitating people to assert these rights through different types of social action and to use them to realize the enormous potential of both the old and new technologies of media and communication, are vital tasks for all concerned people.

We endorse this Statement as an expression of our commitment to communication rights and we further undertake to develop an International Charter on Communication Rights with the widest possible support as a common standard to which every individual and every organ of society should take action to achieve.

Geneva, 11 December 2003

* The most relevant references to communication rights in international human rights instruments.

On the principle of freedom:
Freedom of Expression:
Universal Declaration of Human Rights (1948), Article 19
International Covenant on Civil and Political Rights (1966), Article 19
Convention on the Rights of the Child (1989), Article 13

Protection of privacy:
Universal Declaration of Human Rights (1948), Article 12
International Covenant on Civil and Political Rights (1966), Article 17
Convention on the Rights of the Child (1989), Article 16

On the principle of inclusiveness:
Universal Declaration of Human Rights (1948), Articles 19, 21, 28.
International Covenant on Economic, Social and Cultural Rights (1966), Articles 13, 15.
Declaration of the Principles of International Cultural Co-operation (1966), Article IV (4).

On the principle of diversity:
International Covenant on Civil and Political Rights (1966), Articles 1 (1), 27.
Universal Declaration on Cultural Diversity (1995), Article 5.

On the principle of participation:
Universal Declaration of Human Rights (1948), Articles 21, 27.
International Covenant on Civil and Political Rights (1966), Article 25.

Source : www.communicationrights.org

SELECTIVE GLOSSARY OF KEY TERMS

Advertorials : Also called 'infomercials'; All kinds of editorial pieces or media products produced by advertisers themselves; The practice of inserting advertorials or informercials is a form of dependence of media on advertising business and constitutes a form of self-censorship inflicted by advertising interests.

Agora : An open space where matters concerning the community are discussed. The Greek *agora* was the true 'market place' where ideas were exchanged and decisions made concerning the affairs of state.

Branded : The manufacturer places its name on the product to make it easily identifiable for audiences. The brand name is part of the overall image, encouraging the consumer to believe in the quality of the product and aspire to the life style associated with the brand through advertising.

Communications Revolution : A cycle of ever-accelerating, pervasive and profound cycle of social and cultural changes, even including certain aspects of economy, often attributed to the impact of new media technologies. The new media technologies have added to the media saturation and the media environment is increasingly becoming 'multichannel', 'multi-screened', 'wired' or 'cabled' connected to information super highways This has led to a host of new concepts like digital economy, virtual society, digital divide, etc.

Cultural Capital : Education, knowledge of arts and history provides us a form of capital on which we might build up socially or professionally.

Cultural Homogenization : This term is used to suggest that the media of mass communication are destroying third world cultures and national cultures in specific countries leading to a cultural sameness, standardization or homogenization.

Cultural Imperialism : According to the supporters of this theory the flow of media products such as films and television programmes and other cultural products such as music from the United States and other western countries to the Third World countries is influencing the cultural tastes and habits of the people in these countries. Some people also call it, "Coca-Colanizastion". It is alleged that alongwith texts and popular culutre the values, ideology and beliefs are also being transmitted.

Cultural Invasion : The term refers to one group penetrating the culture of another group to impose its own view of the world.

Cultural shock : An overpowering feeling of anxiety and disorientation that an individual experiences in a new culture.

Cultural Studies : The tradition of research which holds that culture, defined as the totality of human experience, is of fundamental importance for the understanding of human and social behaviour. Study of the media is a part of the cultural studies.

Culture : A collection of beliefs, values and behaviours that are distinctive to a large group of people and are generally expressed through various forms of communication. It is common to visualise culture in terms of nations, but culture can cross national boundaries. Culture is represented through dress, religion and art forms in particular as well as through language. The media present several of these aspects and so also become part of the culture.

Digital : Conversion of information into bits of data for transmission through wire, fiber optic cable, video conference, or other techniques. The method allows simultaneous transmission of voice, data and video.

Disinformation : It is one of the aspects of propaganda which involves tailoring information through distortion, plain lies, selection or economising with truth.

Dollarization : Adoption of the US dollar either formally, as the national currency, or informally, as the main currency across large parts of an economy.

Dual Identity of Newspapers : The two, sometimes conflicting, functions of a newspaper (1) to serve as a quasi-public institution charged with being the watch dog of the public interest and often antagonist of government or other powerful forces, and (2) to make a profit while functioning as a member of the business community.

Entertainment Function : Providing diversion to an audience as opposed to explanation or interpretation. Newspapers amuse and gratify readers with human interest stories and such contents as crossword puzzles, recipes, gardening hints, sports scores and advice.

Glasnost : It refers to the opening up permitted in the Soviet Union from 1989, involving greater freedom of expression.

Global Communication : It refers to the study of transborder transfer of information and data, opinions and values by groups, institutions and governments and the issues that arise from the transfer.

Global Village : 1. The concept introduced by Marshall McLuhan in 1960, it is now used to describe the ways in which modern electronic media have spread around, interconnecting the world and making possible immediate forms of communication.

2. It is a world that is increasingly interconnected by communication technologies and that is tending towards global culture.

Globalization : 1. It describes the widening and deepening of international flows of trade, finance and information in a single, integrated global market. The prescription is to liberalize national and global markets in the belief that free flows of trade, finance and information will produce the best outcome for growth and human welfare. All is presented with an air of inevitability and overwhelming conviction (UNDP, *Human Development Report 1997.*)

2. Consideration of issues from world wide perspective.

Hegemony : It is described as exercise of power by elite groups in a society over the rest of that society. The institutions of media are important in expressing and maintaining that power.

High Technologies : These are capital and energy intensive technologies designed in developed nations to reduce labour and cater to market. In general high technologies have some common features. These create work opportunities for highly trained work forces; they depend on large, centralized, hierarchical organizations that require large capital investments.

Information and Communication Technologies (ICTs) : 1. Refer to the combination of the capacities of information and communication technologies as the central characteristic of the digital era.

2. ICTs refer not only to the Internet, but also to other tools, such as CD-ROM, television, video and (digital) radio and satellite technologies. (CD-ROMs can carry the content of hundreds of Internet sites on a single disk) (*Choices*, June 2000)

Information Societies : The countries in which information workers are more numerous than such occupational categories as farmers, industrial workers or service workers.

Information Workers : The individuals whose main job responsibilities are to gather, process or distribute information, or to produce information technologies like computers or telecommunications equipment that are used by other information workers.

Informational Economy : It is an economy in which sources of productivity and competitiveness for firms, regions, countries depend more than ever on knowledge, information and the technology of their processing, including the technology of management, and the management of technology. The informational economy opens up an extraordinary potential for solving our problems, but because of its dynamism and creativity, it is potentially more exclusionary. (Manuel Castells)

Infotainment : Merging of information and entertainment in news presentation.

Internet : Globally interconnected telecommunication and computer networks systems which allow for diverse forms of interactivity and data interchange. The Internet is making rapid headway even in developing countries like India. It incorporates both the *e-mail and world wide web.*

Internet Fax : Internet fax or fax through Internet is also becoming very popular. This type of fax can be conveyed anywhere in the world at local call rate.

International Communication : The term refers to the study of flow of mediated communication among countries, comparative mass communication systems and communication between national governments.

Internetphilia : The hyped ideology that sees in the Internet the cure for a number of ills besetting the contemporary society. It extends to all aspects of life from academic, finance, politics to civil society.

Kitsch : Art forms that are low quality, unsophisticated, trivial and in bad taste. Many media critics charge that demands for entertainment have resulted in a constant flow of kitsch in the form of popular culture.

Life Styles : This term, which literally means, "style of life", refers broadly to the way people live—which would generally include decisions about how they do up their apartments or homes and more importantly, where these are located; what kind of car they drive or clothes they wear and their mode and style of entertainment and vacation.

Marketing approach to journalism : Approach to journalism that pursues the goal of maximizing profits by selling news as a product, devoting considerable resources to audience research and sharply limiting public service.

Marketisation : The process by which all human activities are structured with in the frame of consumption, production and selling. Transformation of what was originally conceived as public service into a private market whose chief objective is profit.

Mass Culture : This theory suggests the mass media will create a mass society/mass culture in which every one would become a slave like mass man or mass woman, alienated from others and easily manipulated.

McDonaldisation of Society : A process by which the principles of fast food restaurants are coming to dominate more and more sectors of American society as well as that of the rest of the world. It also represents the paradigm of mass homogeneity, sameness and standardisation available at all the McDonald outlets.

Media Power : It refers to the power of media institutions through ownership and control to shape messages which in turn may influence the attitudes and behaviour of the audience.

Media Tycoon : A person who has managed to build a media empire 'single handedly'. Historically it was generally concentrated on one medium, now tycoons own multi-media conglomerates: Some outstanding examples are Rupert Murdoch and Berlusconi.

Merger : A fusion of two or more companies to form one corporate industrial body.

MNCs : Multinational corporations considered to be very large companies with production units in several countries. Several MNCs have made their presence felt in TV, advertising and film production.

Multiculturalism : An attitude of understanding and acceptance among people of different cultures and sub-cultures.

New Media Technologies : The large scale technological development in communication systems and their cultural consequences. The term is also used to refer to cable, satellite and digital and other computer based media in the current phase.

Political Economy : The sociological tradition which analyses society and social phenomena, including media, in terms of the interplay between politics, economy and ideology.

Pornography : The term is rooted in the Greek langauge, *porne,* which means "prostitute". Generally speaking pornography is held to be the material which is sexually explicit and is meant to arouse sexual excitement.

Post modernism : It has been defined as a philosophical system which argues that the old philosophical beliefs that used to guide people are no longer valid. These have been replaced by cultural and social conditions superseding earlier forms of modern twentieth century life. These involve, and result from the rapid growth of media systems and global culture. Some of the post modern films, videos and television programmes reflect the problems and issues encountered by different groups of people—ethnic minorities, women, gays, lesbians etc. These works also help in giving young people identities and belief systems.

Public Sphere : This concept refers to any meeting place, be it physical or virtual, in which people come together as equals for rational discussion of issues for the public good, without the intervention of the forces of the State or of Capital.

RAM : Random Access Memory is the part of the computer's memory which deals with storage of information you are currently working on, which is lost when you close down before saving.

Real-Time : The processing of information that returns a result so rapidly that the interaction appears to be instantaneous. Telephone calls and video-conferencing are examples of real time applications.

Search Engine : It is a website, which once fed with a request for a particular topic gives the addresses of all the websites concerned with the topic. Some popular search engines are Yahoo.com, google, etc.

Socialization : It is a process through which a person becomes a participating member of society. It includes the idea of acquiring beliefs, norms, values and conventions. The media help socialize us.

Subculture : Subculures are cultural sub groups whose religious practices, ethnicity, beliefs, values and lifestyles vary in certain ways from those of the dominant mainstream culture. In any complex society, it is natural to have a number of sub cultures.

Tele-medicine : The practice of using video-conferencing technologies to diagnose illness and provide medical treatment over a distance.

Telecommuting : The process of commuting to work electronically rather than physically. Telecommuting will find greater acceptance as the public–switched telephone network beomes more robust and digital and as video conferencing and multi media technologies arrive at the desktop.

Technological Determinism : It is an approach that considers technology as the main cause of social change.

Technology : 1. Technology has been taken from the Greek language, 'Techno' means art of doing or systematic way of working where as 'logus' means knowledge or study.

So technology is used for all those procedures or systematic ways of working by application of scientific laws.

2. Technology refers to both the hardware, viz. machines, equipment and software such as programmes or procedure of working or running machines.

3. It is defined as information that is put to use in order to accomplish some task.

Upload : Any information which is posted on the Internet is called uploading.

URL : It stands for Uniform Resource Locator. It means the address of a particular website, e.g. www.times of india.com.

Virtual Community : The idea that communities of interest/action can now be built using the Internet, their distinction being a lack of dependence on physical proximity and the possibility of operating across multiple international boundaries.

Wan : Wide Area Network. A communication network that services a geographical area larger than that served by a local network or metropolitan area network. WANs include commercial or educational dial-up networks.

Web Page : Web page in the single page of a website. A web site may contain hundreds or thousands of web pages depending upon its size. Web page is the basic unit of web site.

Youth Culture : Youth cultures are sub-cultures formed by young people around some area of interest, usually connected with leisure and entertainment—for example, surfing, rock music or some aspects of computers (games, hacking). Members of the youth culture develop distinctive ways of dressing and develop instituions that cater to their needs.

GLOSSARY OF SELECTED ICT TERMS

ARPANet – (Advanced Research Projects Agency Network): The precursor to the *Internet*. Developed in the late 60s and early 70s by the US Department of Defense as an experiment in wide-area-networking to connect together computers that were each running different system so that people at one location could use computing resources from another location.

Backbone: A high-speed line or series of connections that forms a major pathway within a network. The term is relative as a backbone in a small *network* will likely be much smaller than many non-backbone lines in a large network.

Bandwidth: How much stuff you can send through a connection. Usually measured in bits-per-second. A full page of English text is about 16,000 bits. A fast modem can move about 57,000 bits in one second. Full-motion full-screen video would require roughly 10,000,000 bits-per-second, depending on compression.

Binary: Information consisting entirely of ones and zeros. Also, commonly used to refer to files that are not simply text files, e.g. images.

Bit : (Binary DigIT): A single digit number in base-2, in other words, either a 1 or a 0. The smallest unit of computerized data. *Bandwidth* is usually measured in bits-per-second.

Blog : (weB LOG): A blog is basically a journal that is available on the *web*. The activity of updating a blog is "blogging" and someone who keeps a blog is a "blogger." Blogs are typically updated daily using software that allows people with little or no technical background to update and maintain the blog.

bps : (Bits-Per-Second): A measurement of how fast data is moved from one place to another. A 56K *modem* can move about 57,000 bits per second.

Browser: A *Client* program (software) that is used to look at various kinds of Internet resources.

Byte: A set of Bits that represent a single character. Usually there are 8 Bits in a Byte, sometimes more, depending on how the measurement is being made.

Cyberpunk: Cyberpunk was originally a cultural sub-genre of science fiction taking place in a not-so-distant, dystopian, over-industrialized society. The term grew out of the work of William Gibson and Bruce Sterling and has evolved into a cultural label encompassing many different kinds of human, machine, and punk attitudes. It includes clothing and lifestyle choices as well.

Cyberspace: Term originated by author William Gibson in his novel *Neuromancer*, the word Cyberspace is currently used to describe the whole range of information resources available through computer networks.

Digerati: The digital version of literati, it is a reference to a vague crowd of people seen to be knowledgeable, hip, or otherwise in-the-know in regard to the digital revolution.

DNS – (Domain Name System): The Domain Name System is the system that translates Internet *domain names* into *IP numbers*. A "DNS Server" is a *server* that performs this kind of translation.

Domain Name: The unique name that identifies an Internet site. Domain Names always have 2 or more parts, separated by dots. The part on the left is the most specific, and the part on the right is the most general. A given machine may have more than one Domain Name but a given Domain Name points to only one machine. For example, some of the domain names are:

matisse.net
mail.matisse.net
workshop.matisse.net

Download: Transferring data (usually a file) from a another computer to the computer you are are using. The opposite of *upload*.

Email – (Electronic Mail): Messages, usually text, sent from one person to another via computer. E-mail can also be sent automatically to a large number of addresses.

FAQ – (Frequently Asked Questions): FAQs are documents that list and answer the most common questions on a particular subject. There are hundreds of FAQs on subjects as diverse as Pet Grooming and Cryptography. FAQs are usually written by people who are tired of answering the same question over and over.

Fire Wall: A combination of hardware and software that separates a *Network* into two or more parts for security purposes.

Flame War: When an online discussion degenerates into a series of personal attacks against the debators, rather than discussion of their positions. A heated exchange.

Gateway: The technical meaning is a hardware or software set-up that translates between two dissimilar protocols, for example America Online has a gateway that translates between its internal, proprietary e-mail format and Internet e-mail format. Another, sloppier meaning of gateway is to describe any mechanism for providing access to another system, e.g. AOL might be called a gateway to the Internet.

GIF – (Graphic Interchange Format): A common format for image files, especially suitable for images containing large areas of the same color. GIF format files of simple images are often smaller than the same file would be if stored in *JPEG* format, but GIF format does not store photographic images as well as JPEG.

Gigabyte: 1000 or 1024 *Megabytes*, depending on who is measuring.

Hit: As used in reference to the World Wide Web, ?hit? means a single request from a web *browser* for a single item from a web server; thus in order for a web browser to display a page that contains 3 graphics, 4 ?hits? would occur at the server: 1 for the HTML page, and one for each of the 3 graphics.

Home Page (or Homepage): Several meanings. Originally, the web page that your browser is set to use when it starts up. The more common meaning refers to the main web page for a business, organization, person or simply the main page out of a collection of web pages, e.g. "Check out so-and-so's new Home Page."

Host: Any computer on a *network* that is a repository for services available to other computers on the network. It is quite common to have one host machine provide several services, such as *SMTP* (email) and *HTTP* (web).

HTML – (HyperText Markup Language): The coding language used to create Hypertext documents for use on the *World Wide Web*. HTML looks a lot like old-fashioned typesetting code, where you surround a block of text with codes that indicate how it should appear.

The "hyper" in Hypertext comes from the fact that in HTML you can specify that a block of text, or an image, is linked to another file on the Internet. HTML files are meant to be viewed using a "Web Browser".

HTML is loosely based on a more comprehensive system for markup called SGML.

HTTP – (HyperText Transfer Protocol): The protocol for moving *hypertext*files across the *Internet*. Requires a HTTP *client* program on one end, and an HTTP *server* program on the other end. HTTP is the most important protocol used in the *World Wide Web* (WWW).

Hypertext: Generally, any text that contains links to other documents—words or phrases in the document that can be chosen by a reader and which cause another document to be retrieved and displayed.

Internet: The vast collection of inter-connected networks that are connected using the *TCP/IP* protocols and that evolved from the *ARPANET* of the late 60s and early 70s.

The Internet connects tens of thousands of independent networks into a vast global Internet and is probably the largest *Wide Area Network* in the world.

Intranet: A private *network* inside a company or organization that uses the same kinds of software that you would find on the public *Internet*, but that is only for internal use.

IP Number – (Internet Protocol Number): Sometimes called a dotted quad. A unique number consisting of 4 parts separated by dots, e.g.

IRC – (Internet Relay Chat): Basically a huge multi-user live chat facility. There are a number of major IRC *servers* around the world which are linked to each other. Anyone can create a channel and anything that anyone types in a given channel is seen by all others in the channel. Private channels can (and are) created for multi-person conference calls.

ISDN – (Integrated Services Digital Network): Basically a way to move more data over existing regular phone lines. ISDN is available to much of the USA and in most markets it is priced very comparably to standard analog phone circuits. It can provide speeds of roughly 128,000 bits-per-second over regular phone lines. In practice, most people will be limited to 56,000 or 64,000 bits-per-second.

Unlike *DSL,* ISDN can be used to connect to many different locations, one at a time, just like a regular telephone call, as long the other location also has ISDN.

ISP – (Internet Service Provider): An institution that provides access to the Internet in some form, usually for money.

Java: Java is a network-friendly programming language invented by Sun Microsystems.

Java is often used to build large, complex systems that involve several different computers interacting across networks, for example transaction processing systems. Java is also becoming popular for creating programs that run in small electronic devices, such as mobile telephones.

Kilobyte: A thousand bytes. Actually, usually 1024 (2^{10}) bytes.

LAN – (Local Area Network): A computer network limited to the immediate area, usually the same building or floor of a building.

Leased Line: Refers to line such as a telephone line or fiber-optic cable that is rented for exclusive 24 hour, 7 days-a-week use from your location to another location. The highest speed data connections require a leased line.

Login: The act of connecting to a computer system by giving your credentials (usually your "username" and "password")

Maillist (or Mailing List): A (usually automated) system that allows people to send *e-mail* to one address, whereupon their message is copied and sent to all of the other subscribers to the maillist. In this way, people who have many different kinds of e-mail access can participate in discussions together.

Megabyte: A million *bytes*. Actually, technically, 1024 *kilobytes*.

Modem – (MOdulator, DEModulator): A device that connects a computer to a phone line. A telephone for a computer. A modem allows a computer to talk to other computers through the phone system. Basically, modems do for computers what a telephone does for humans.

Netiquette: The etiquette on the *Internet*.

Netizen:Derived from the term citizen, referring to a citizen of the *Internet*, or someone who uses networked resources. The term connotes civic responsibility and participation.

Netscape: A *WWW Browser* and the name of a company. The Netscape (tm) browser was originally based on the *Mosaic* program developed at the National Center for Supercomputing Applications (NCSA).

Network: Any time you connect 2 or more computers together so that they can share resources, you have a computer network. Connect 2 or more networks together and you have an *Internet*.

Newsgroup: The name for discussion groups on *USENET*.

Password: A code used to gain access (*login*) to a locked system. Good passwords contain letters and non-letters and are not simple combinations such as *virtue7*.

Portal: Usually used as a marketing term to describe a Website that is or is intended to be the first place people see when using the Web. Typically a "Portal site" has a catalog of websites, a search engine, or both. A Portal site may also offer email and other service to entice people to use that site as their main "point of entry" (hence "portal") to the Web.

Search Engine: A (usually web-based) system for searching the information available on the *Web*.

Some search engines work by automatically searching the contents of other systems and creating a database of the results. Other search engines contain only material manually approved for inclusion in a database, and some combine the two approaches.

Server: A computer, or a software package, that provides a specific kind of service to *client* software running on other computers. The term can refer to a particular piece of software, such as a *WWW* server, or to the machine on which the software is running, e.g. "Our mail server is down today, that's why e-mail isn't getting out."

A single server machine can (and often does) have several different server software packages running on it, thus providing many different servers to *clients* on the *network*.

Sometimes server software is designed so that additional capabilities can be added to the main program by adding small programs known as *servlets*.

Spam (or Spamming): An inappropriate attempt to use a *mailing list*, or *USENET* or other networked communications facility as if it was a broadcast medium (which it is not) by sending the same message to a large number of people who didn't ask for it. The term probably comes from a famous Monty Python skit which featured the word spam repeated over and over. The term may also have come from someone's low opinion of the food product with the same name, which is generally perceived as a generic content-free waste of resources. (Spam® is a registered trademark of Hormel Corporation, for its processed meat product.)

Terminal: A device that allows you to send commands to a computer somewhere else. At a minimum, this usually means a keyboard and a display screen and some simple circuitry. Usually you will use terminal software in a personal computer—the software pretends to be (emulates) a physical terminal and allows you to type commands to a computer somewhere else.

Trojan Horse: A computer programme is either hidden inside another programme or that masquerades as something it is not in order to trick potential users into running it. For example a programme that appears to be a game or image file but in reality performs some other function. The term "Trojan Horse" comes from a possibly mythical use of war used by the Greeks sometime between 1500 and 1200 B.C.

A Trojan Horse computer programme may spread itself by sending copies of itself from the host computer to other computers, but unlike a *virus* it will (usually) not infect other programmes.

Upload: Transferring data (usually a file) from the computer you are using to another computer. The opposite of *download*.

URL – (Uniform Resource Locator): The term URL is basically synonymous with *URI*. URI has replaced URL in technical specifications.

Virus: A chunk of computer programming code that makes copies of itself without any concious human intervention. Some viruses do more than simply replicate themselves, they might display messages, install other software or files, delete software of files, etc.

A virus requires the presence of some other program to replicate itself. Typically viruses spread by attaching themselves to programs and in some cases files, for example the file formats for Microsoft word processor and spreadsheet programs allow the inclusion of programs called "macros" which can in some cases be a breeding ground for viruses.

WAN – (Wide Area Network): Any *Internet* or *network* that covers an area larger than a single building or campus.

Web: Short for "World Wide Web."

Web page: A document designed for viewing in a *web browser*. Typically written in *HTML*. A *website* is made of one or more web pages.

Website: The entire collection of *web pages* and other information (such as images, sound, and video files, etc.) that are made available through what appears to users as a single web server. Typically all of the pages in a website share the same basic *URL*, for example the following URLs are all for pages within the same website:

http://www.baytherapy.com/
http://www.baytherapy.com/whatis/
http://www.baytherapy.com/teenagers/

The term has a somewhat informal nature since a large organization might have separate "websites" for each division, but someone might talk informally about the organizations' "website" when speaking of all of them.

WWW – (World Wide Web): World Wide Web (or simply Web for short) is a term frequently used (incorrectly) when referring to "The Internet",

---

Source : www.matisse.net

BIBLIOGRAPHY

Ten Recommended Texts

For students who wish to go in for further reading on international communication I suggest the follwoing as useful texts which cover related issues. This list clearly represents a personal view and is not an objective judgement.

Asian Media Information and Communication Centre (1996) *Opening Windows : Issues in Communication,* Singapore.

Briggs Asa and Peter Burke (2002) *A Social History of The Media : From Gutenberg to the Internet;* Polity, www.polity.co.uk.

David Held and Anthony McGrew (2003) *The Global Transformations Reader : An Introduction to the Globalization Debate,* Polity, www.polity.co.uk

David Miller (2004) (ed) *Tell me Lies : Propaganda and Media Distortion in the Attack on Iraq, Pluto Press, London.*

Dicken, Peter (1998) *Global Shift : Transforming the World Economy,* Paul Chapman Publishing Ltd, London.

Donald Read (1992) *The Power of News : The History of Reuters,* Oxford University Press.

Giddens, Anthony (2000) *Runaway World : How Globalisation is reshaping our lives,* Profile Books, London.

Newbold Chris, Boyd—Barrett Oliver, and Hilde Van Den Bulck (eds) (2002) *The Media Book* www.arnoldpublishers. com

UNESCO (1982) *Many Voices, One World :* Report of The International Commission on the Study of Communication Problems, Paris.

Webster, Frank (ed) (2004) *The Information Society Reader,* Routledge London.

Books and Journals

Barker, C (1997) *Global Television: An Introduction,* Blackwell publishers, UK.

Berger, Arthur Asa (2003), *Media and Society: A Critical Perspective.* The R&L Series in Mass Communication, Rowman & Littlefield Publishers, Inc, Oxford, UK.

British Council (2001) *A Manual of Human Rights Reporting in India, Press and People,* New Delhi.

Charles Handy (2001) *The Elephant and the Flea: Looking Backwards to the Future,* Hutchinson, London.

Curran, J. (ed) (2000) *Media Organisations in Society,* Arnold, www.arnoldpublishers. com

David McQueen (1998) *Television : A Media Student's Guide,* Arnold, London.

Don Tapscott (1998) *Growing up Digital : The Rise of the Net Generation.* McGraw Hill, New York.

Frances Cairncross (1977), *The Death of Distance,* Harvard Business School Press, Boston, Massachusters.

Human Rights : The New Consensus (1994), Regency Press, Golden House, London.

Ian Angell (2000) *The New Barbarian Manifesto : How to Survive the Information Age,* Kogan page, London.

Ian Shircore and Richard London (1999) *Mastering the Internet,* Orion Business Books, 4 upper St.Martin's Lane, London.

James Curran and Jean Seaton (2003) *Power without Responsibility, The press, broadcasting and new media in Britain,* Routledge, London.

James Watson (2003) *Media Communication : An Introduction to Theory and Process,* Palgrave Macmillan. Houndsmill, Hampshire, www.palgrave.com

Jandt, Fred Edmund (2001) *Intercultural Communication : An Introduction,* Sage Publications, Thousand Oaks, California.

Jerry Everard (2000) *Virtual States : The Internet and Boundaries of the Nation-State,* Routledge, London.

Leon Kreitzman (1999) *The 24 Hour Society,* Profile Books London. www.profilebooks.co.uk.

Marsha Jones and Emma Jones (1999) *Mass Media,* Macmillan Press, Houndmills, Bansingstoke, Hampshire.

McNair Brian (2003) *News Journalism in the UK*, Routledge, London.

Melkote, Srinivas R. and H. Laslie Steeves (2001), *Communication and Development in the Third World : Theory and Practice*, Sage Publication, New Delhi.

Paul Kingsnorth (2003) *One No, Many Yeses : A Journey to the Heart of the Global Resistance Movement*, Simon & Schuster UK Ltd, London.

Rob Waugh and Celia Walden (2004) "The Hit Factory and Search for Me in Night & Day", *The Mail on Sunday* : 4 April. London.

Tim O'Sullivan, Brian Dutton, Philip Rayner (1998) *Studying the Media*, Arnold, London.

Time (2003) 13 October *The BEEB takes on the World* : The BEEB Worldwide : How the best known public service broadcaster learned to love capitalism.

UNDP (2000) Human Development Report, *Human Rights and Human Development*, Oxford University Press, Oxford.

We are everywhere, (2003) *The irresistible rise of global anticapitalism* edited by Notes from Nowhere, Verso London.

World Bank (1998/99), *World Development Report*, Knowledge for Development, Oxford University Press, Oxford.

World Bank (2000) *World Development Report 1999/2000 Entering the 21st century*, Oxford University Press.

Websites

www.arnoldpublishers.com
www.baytherapy.com/
www.communicationrights.org
www.google.com
www.intellectual-property.gov.uk
www.kogan-page.co.uk.
www.palgrave.com
www.polity.co.uk
www.profilebooks.co.uk.
www.search.msn.com
www.un.org

Author's e-mail:
vijaya06102003@yahoo.co.uk

INDEX

SOME OPINIONS ON AUTHOR'S PUBLICATIONS AND WORK

Communication Development and Civil Society

The author really deserves unqualified praise for timely bringing out the book on the issues which are of national importance. Hence this publication is sure to attract the attention of wider audience. It highlights the fact that the role of voluntary organizations can bring a sea change in the overall status of society. The primary objective of the book appears to exhort Government, the private sector, civil society and donor organizations to work in unison for a broad based development. The book is certainly useful not only for the voluntary organisations, representatives of funding agencies, development functionaries but also for those who are involved and interested in the issues of human development, human rights, planning, rural development, gender justice, social development and justice.

(*Kurukeshtra,* Vol. 52, No. 6; April 2004)

The topic is of current and continuing interest. The value of the publication is enhanced by your use of the latest census data and the trouble you have taken to revise, enlarge and update the text. The book should be a valuable resource for students of mass communication in India.

I congratulate you on your commendable contribution to the literature on mass communication in India and wish you continued success in your efforts.

Vijay Menon, Former Secretary General,
Asian Media, Information and Communication Centre,
Singapore.

Hand book of Journalism and Mass Communication **with Vir Bala Aggarwal and** ***Handbook of Reporting and Communication Skills***

Thanks a lot for sending a copy each of your books : *Handbook of Journalism and Mass Communication* and a *Handbook of Reporting and Communication Skills.* I am going through these books and I am impressed by the content design. I am sure these books will come in very handy to university students and scholars of mass communication and journalism.

Prof. Umakant Misra,
Director Publications Division
Ministry of Information and Broadcasting,
Government of India

* * * * * * * * *

"I think you deserve the greatest compliments from the media persons whom you are bestowing with a book every year. This being your eighth book, you seem to have outstripped all those who have produced books on a variety of media subjects. It is indeed an excellent contribution and should be of immense use to media students, researchers and teachers. In fact, very few media teachers are as professional or prolific book writers as you are ... Congratulations and my best wishes for your powerful pen."

Prof. M.R. Dua,
Former Professor, IIMC, New Delhi,
Nodal Person, UGC, CDC in Mass Communication

"Thanks for sending me a bunch of your books. I will enjoy and profit by reading them. No Indian teacher has written so many books on Communication.
Please accept my heartiest congratulations."

Prof. Anjan Kumar Banerji,
(Padamshri)
Emeritus Fellow, UGC
Formerly Prof. & Head,
Deptt. of Journalism and Mass Communication,
BHU, Varanasi